# The Adventures of Bella Noelle

Hey guys it's Bella and I am so glad you decided to join me on another adventure. In this workbook, we will learn about the numbers 1-10. We will count our numbers, write our numbers, play fun games with our numbers, and so much more. So come on guys let's get going on our adventure!

# Coloring Numbers

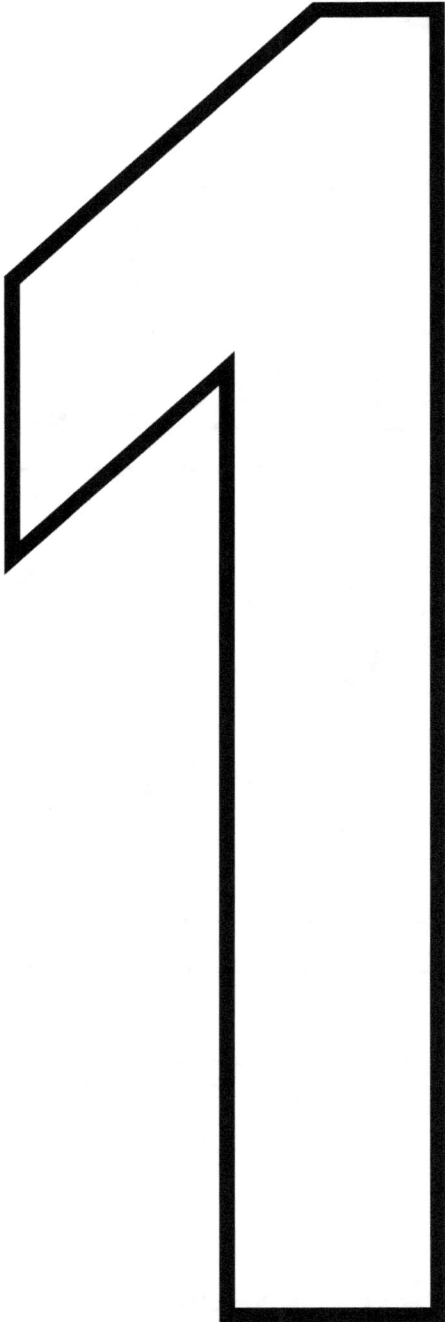

1

# Writing Numbers

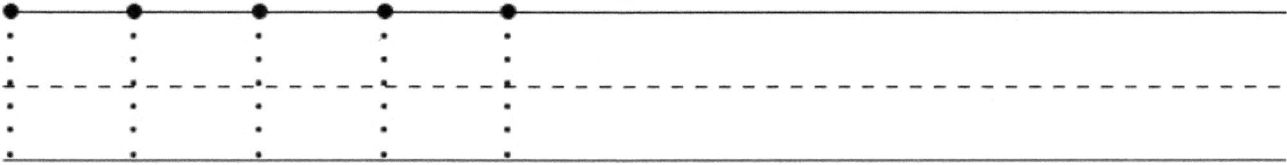

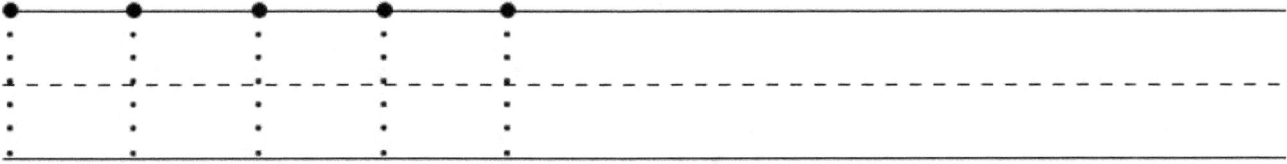

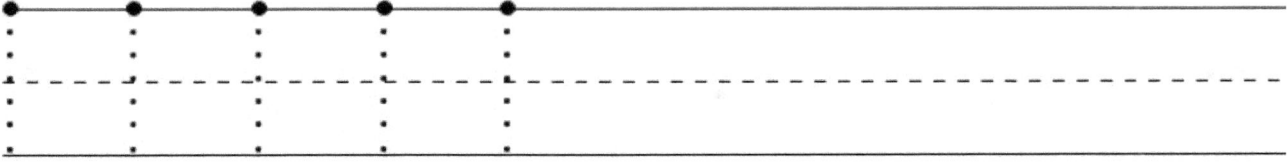

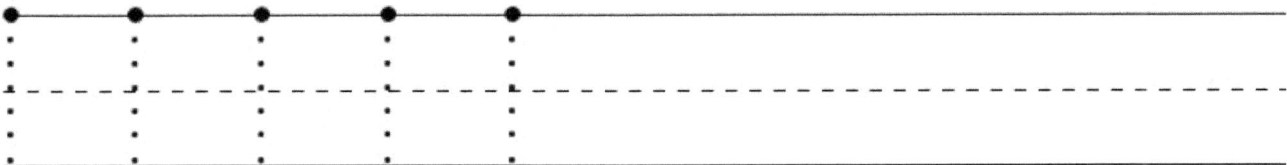

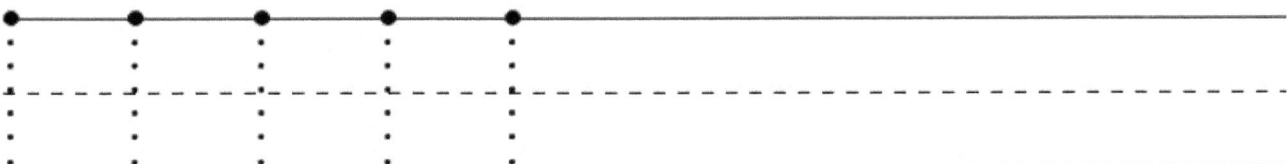

I

# Writing Number Words

# one

one one one

one one one

one one one

one one one

one one one

one one one

one one one

# Writing Numbers

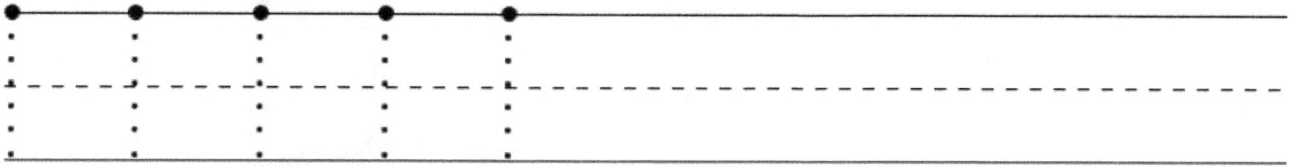

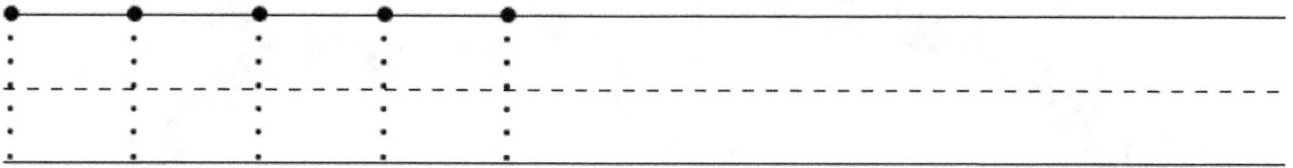

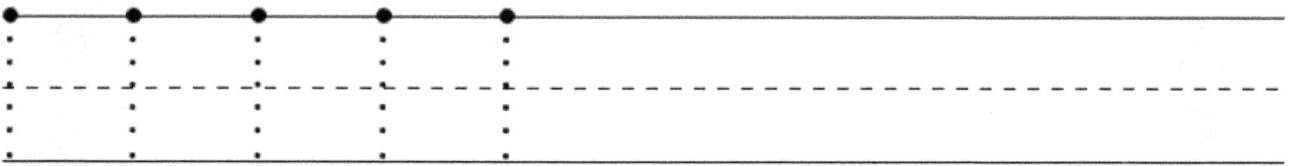

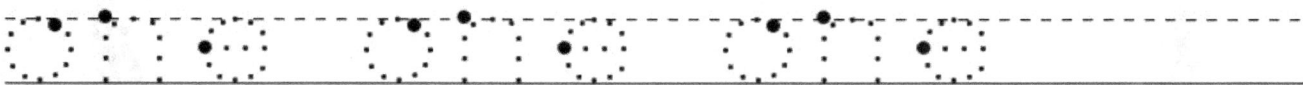

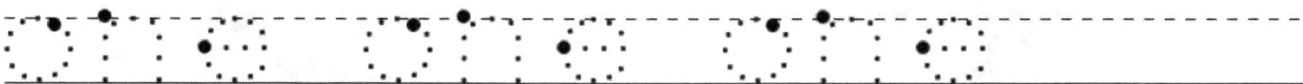

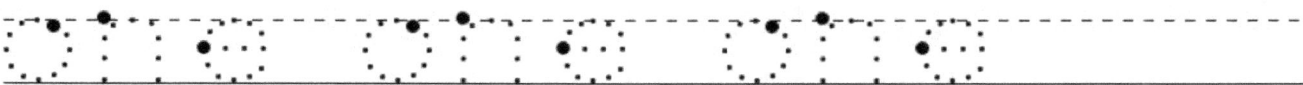

1 1 1 1 1

1 1 1 1 1

1 1 1 1 1

one one one

one one one

one one one

Coloring Objects

one

# Count and Label

# Count and Label

_____

_____

_____

_____

DIRECTIONS: TRACE THE WORDS AND NUMBERS BELOW.

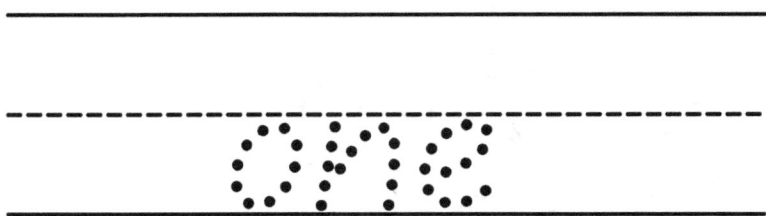

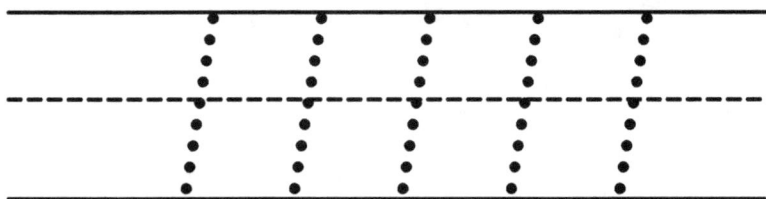

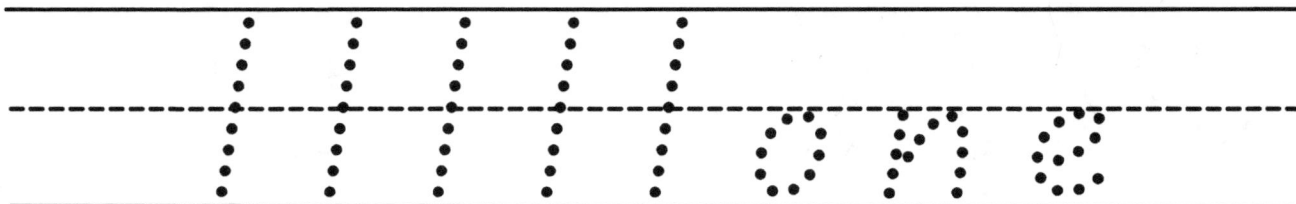

one

1 1 1 1 1

1 1 1 1 1 one

COLOR ONE STAR:

CIRCLE THE ONES:

| 1 | 3 | 5 |
|---|---|---|
| 4 | 2 | 1 |
| 6 | 1 | 8 |
| 1 | 7 | 1 |
| 2 | 1 | 4 |

# Number Hunt

## Find and color number 1

# Coloring Numbers

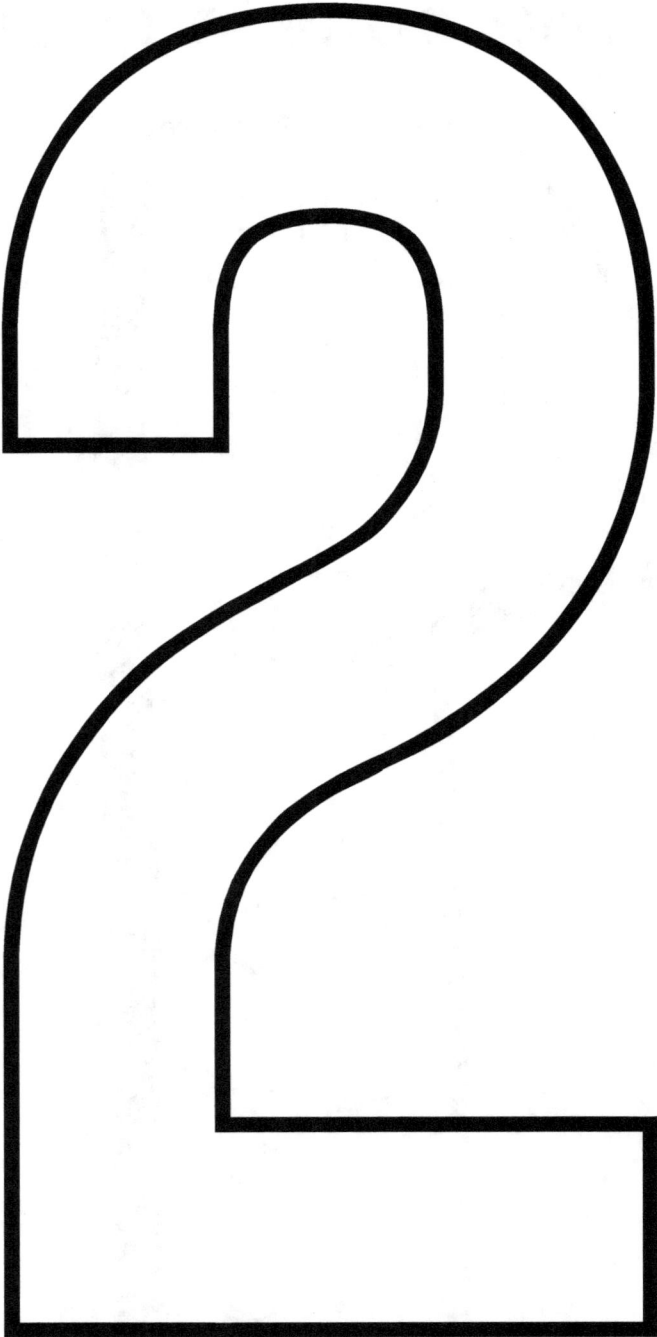

2

# Writing Numbers

2

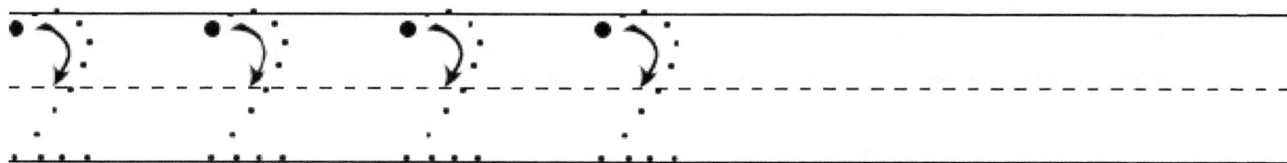

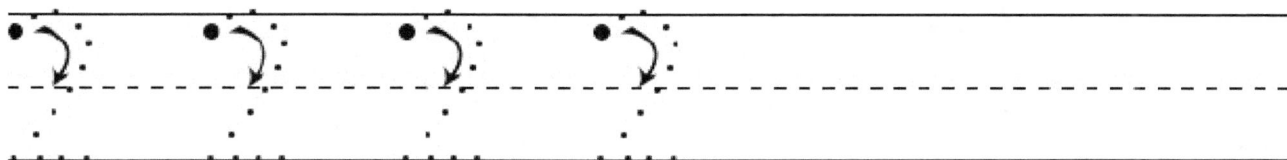

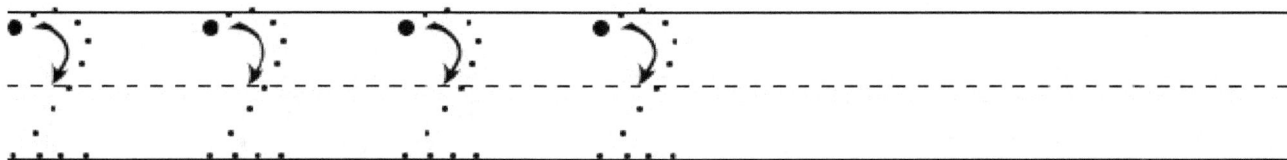

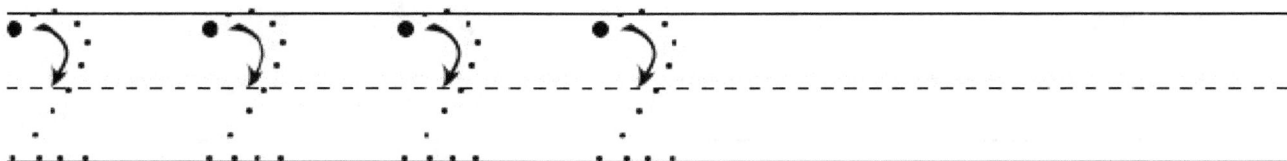

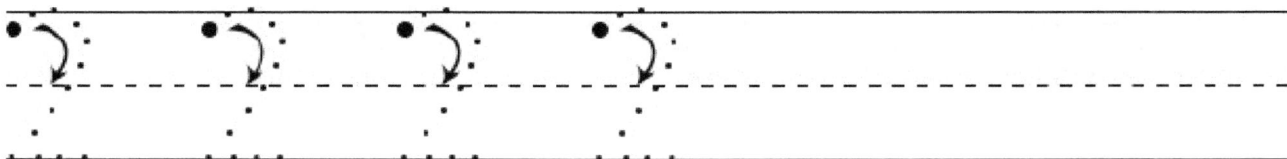

# Writing Number Words

two

two two two

two two two

two two two

two two two

two two two

two two two

# Writing Numbers

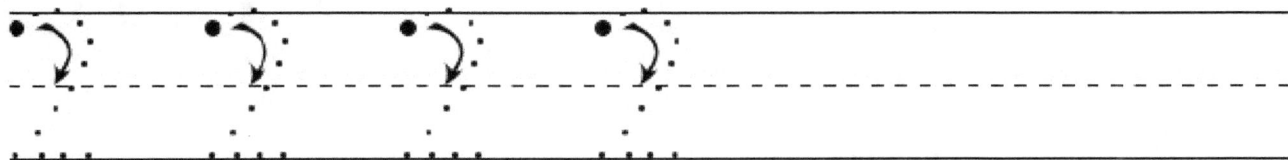

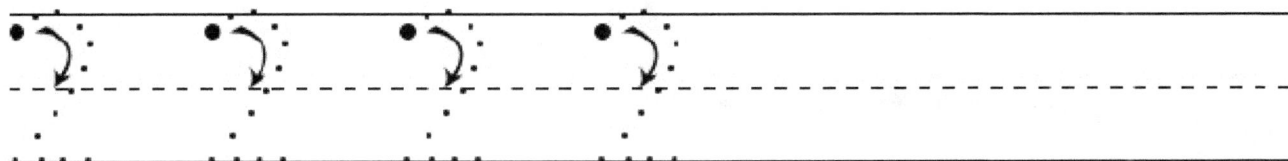

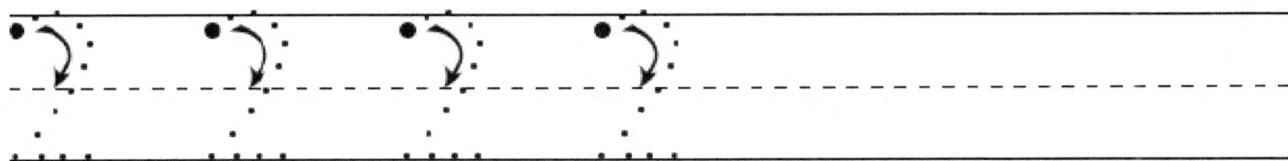

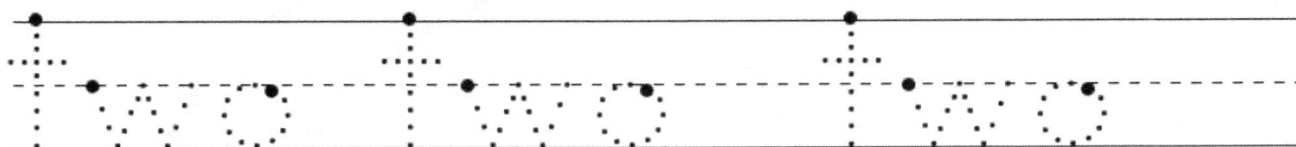

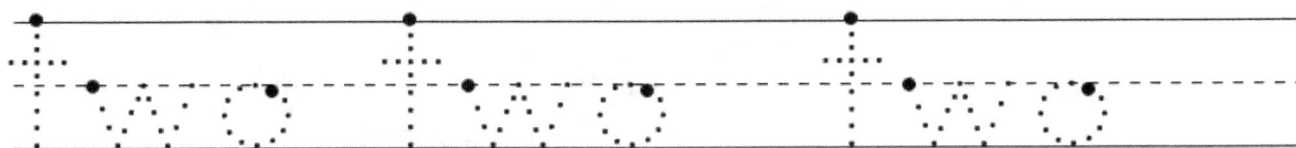

2 2 2 2

2 2 2 2

2 2 2 2

two   two   two

two   two   two

two   two   two

Coloring Objects

two

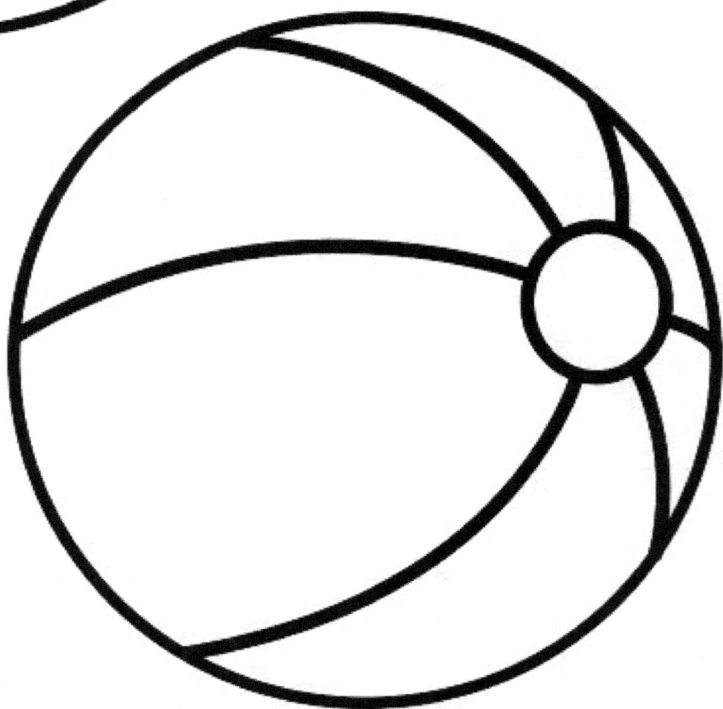

DIRECTIONS: TRACE THE WORDS AND NUMBERS BELOW.

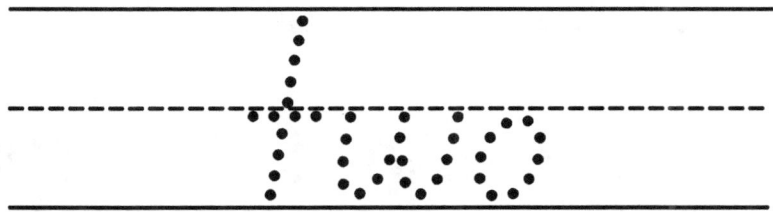

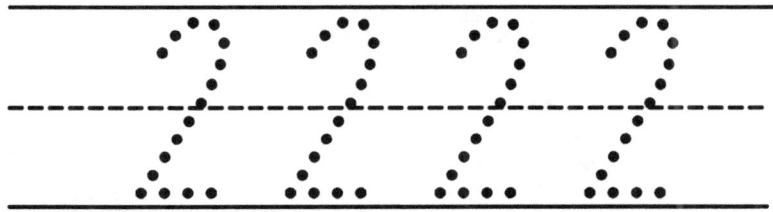

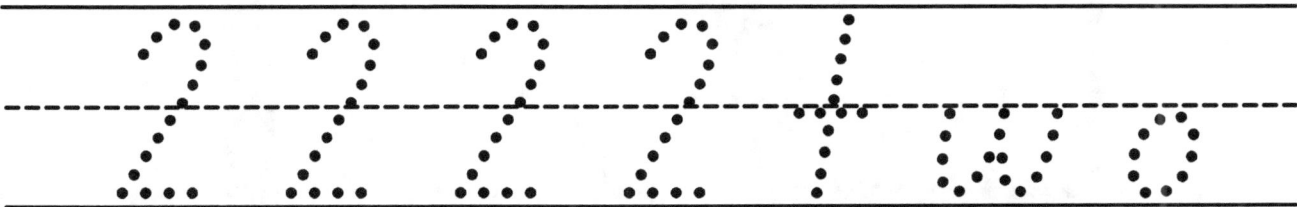

2

two

2 2 2 2

2 2 2 2 two

COLOR TWO TRIANGLES:

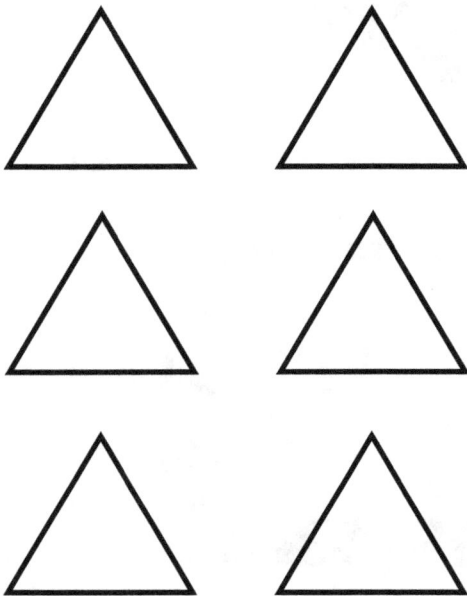

CIRCLE THE TWOS:

| 2 | 3 | 5 |
|---|---|---|
| 4 | 2 | 1 |
| 6 | 1 | 2 |
| 1 | 2 | 1 |
| 2 | 1 | 4 |

# Number Hunt

## Find and color number 2

# Coloring Numbers

# Writing Numbers

## 3

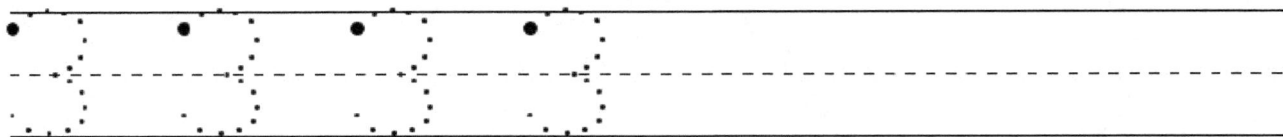

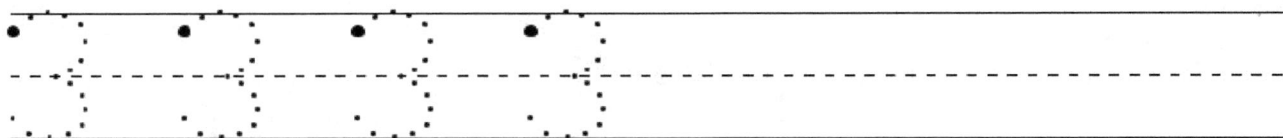

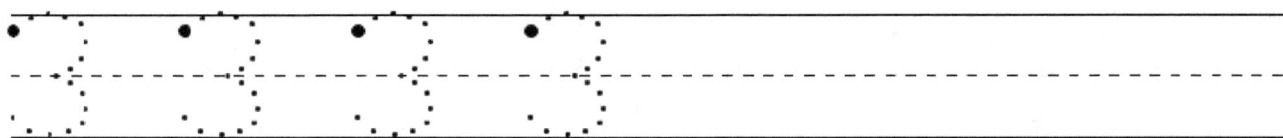

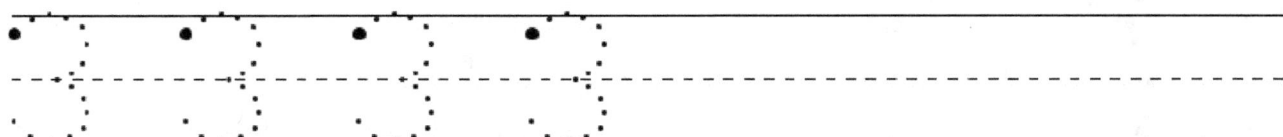

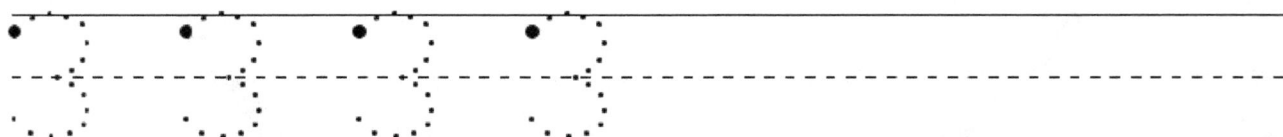

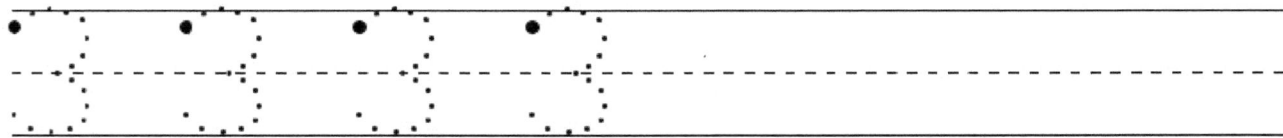

# Writing Number Words

# three

three three

three three

three three

three three

three three

three three

# Writing Numbers

3 3 3 3

3 3 3 3

3 3 3 3

three three

three three

three three

# Coloring Objects

# three

# Dot-to-Dot

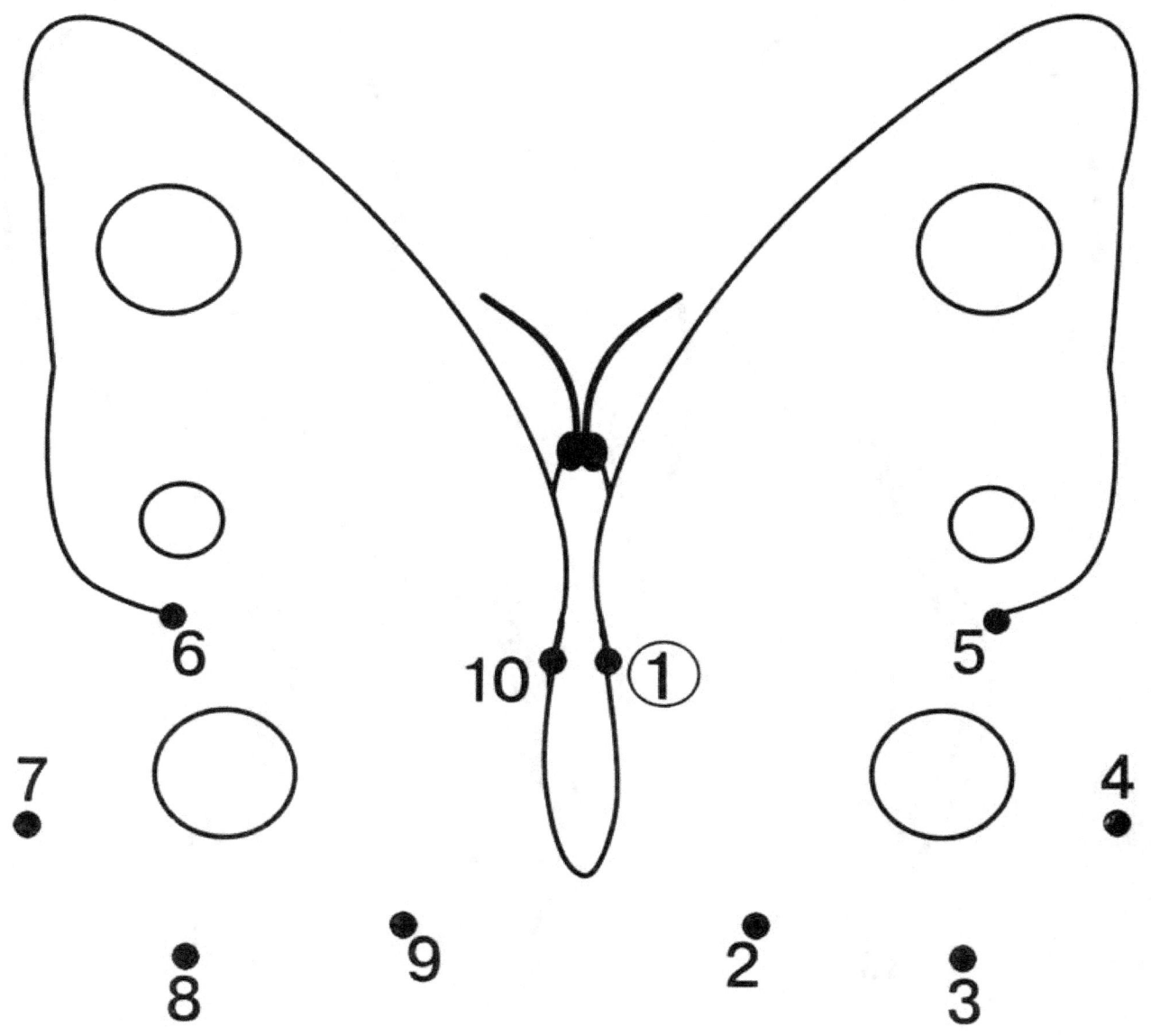

# DIRECTIONS: TRACE THE WORDS AND NUMBERS BELOW.

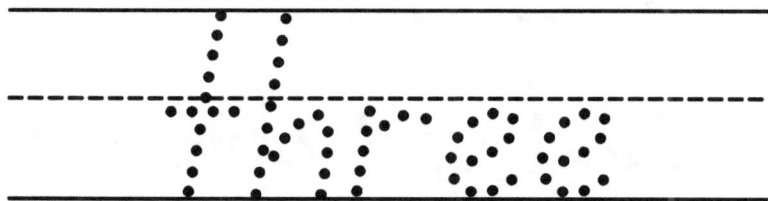

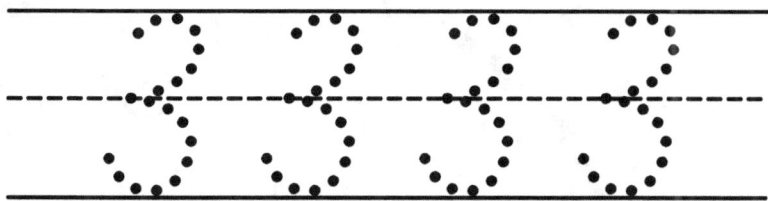

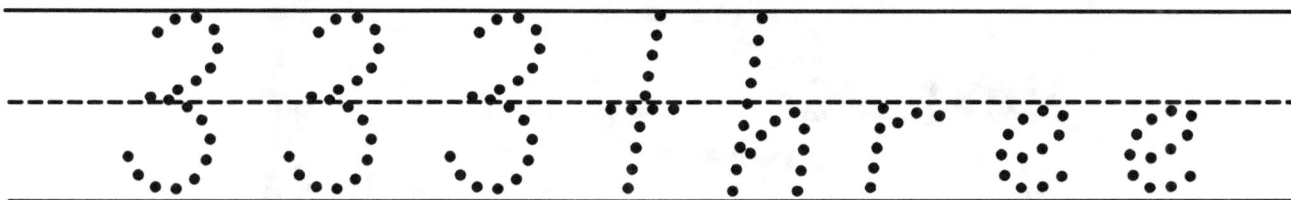

**3**

three

3 3 3 3

3 3 3 three

## COLOR THREE SQUARES:

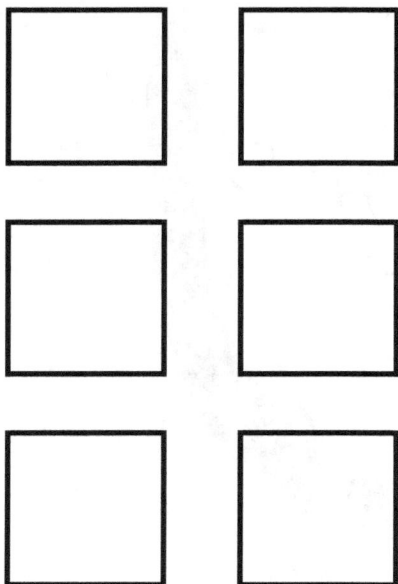

## CIRCLE THE THREES:

| | | |
|---|---|---|
| 2 | 3 | 5 |
| 4 | 2 | 3 |
| 3 | 1 | 2 |
| 3 | 5 | 1 |
| 6 | 3 | 4 |

# Number Hunt

## Find and color number 3

# Coloring Numbers

4

# Writing Numbers

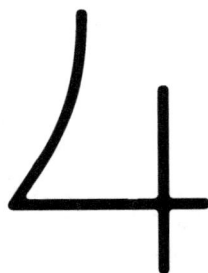

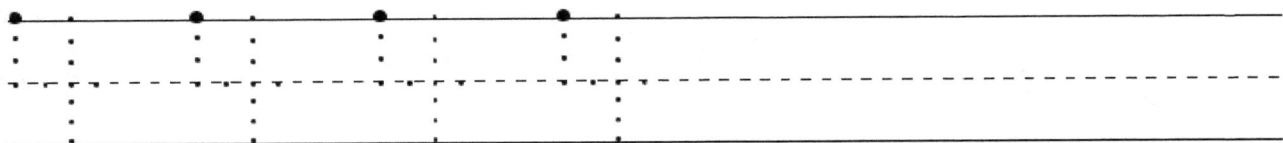

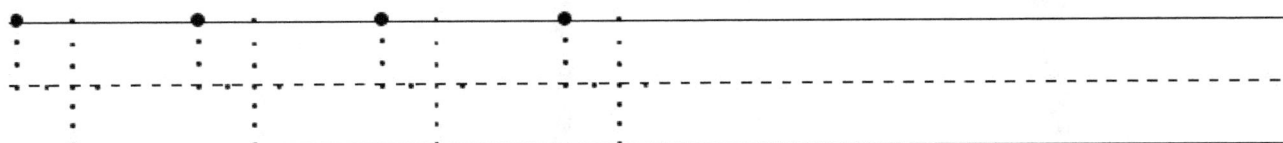

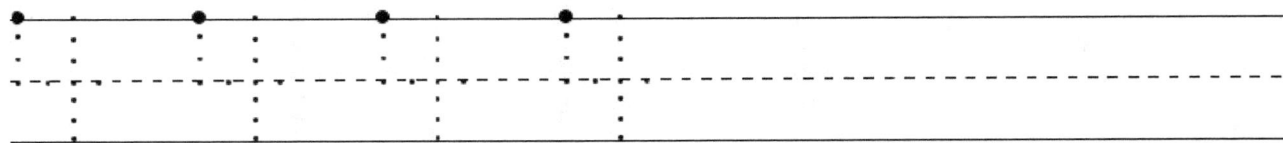

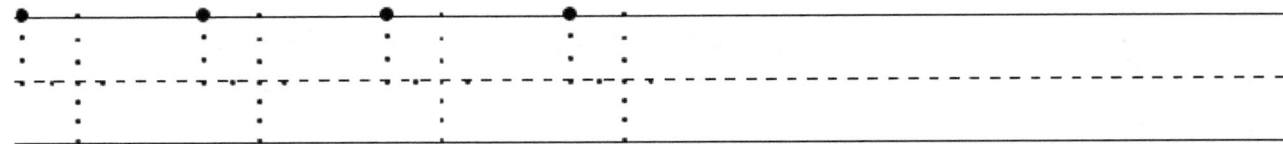

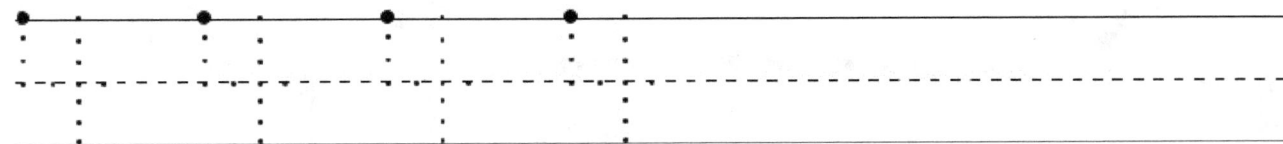

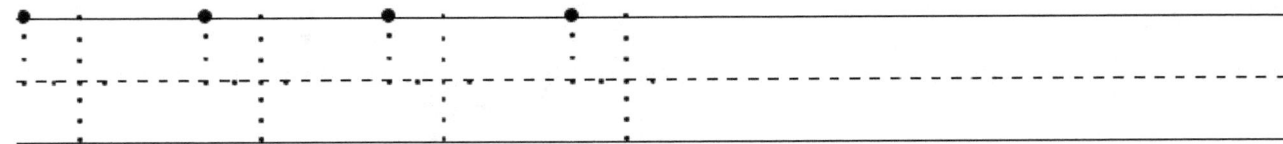

4

# Writing Number Words

# four

four    four    four

four    four    four

four    four    four

four    four    four

four    four    four

four    four    four

four    four    four

# Writing Numbers

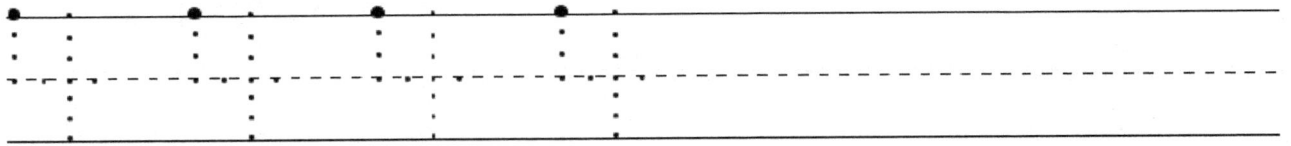

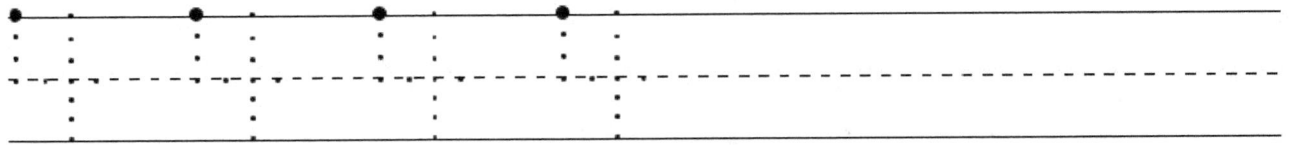

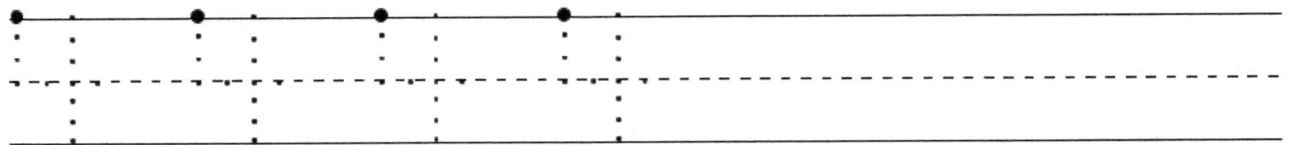

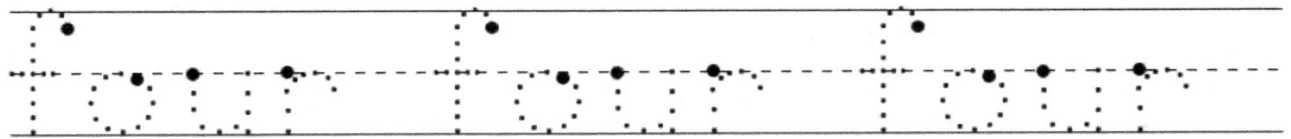

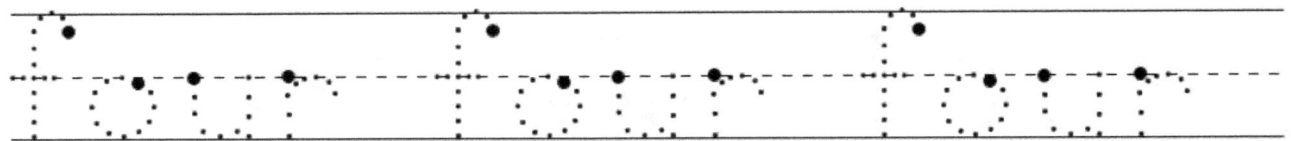

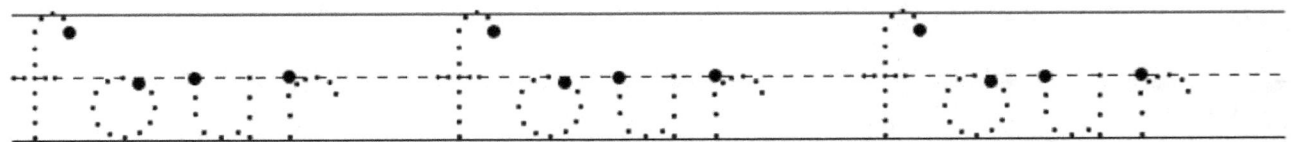

4 4 4 4

4 4 4 4

4 4 4 4

four four four

four four four

four four four

# Coloring Objects

# four

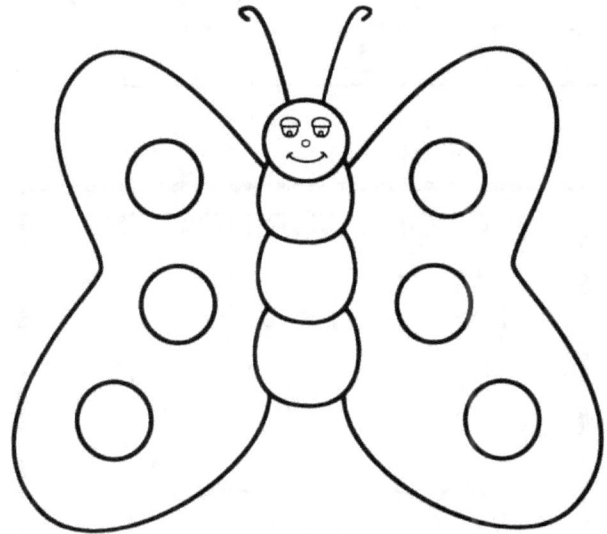

# DIRECTIONS: TRACE THE WORDS AND NUMBERS BELOW.

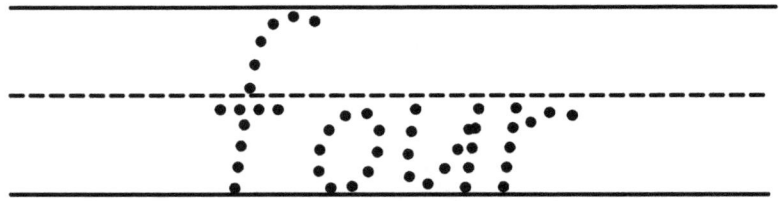

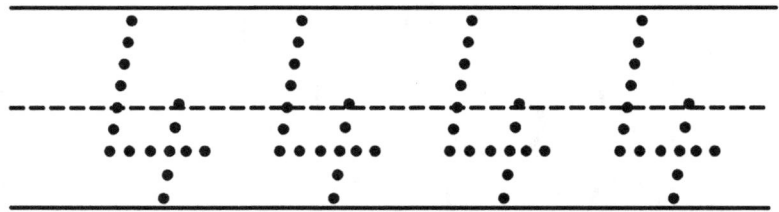

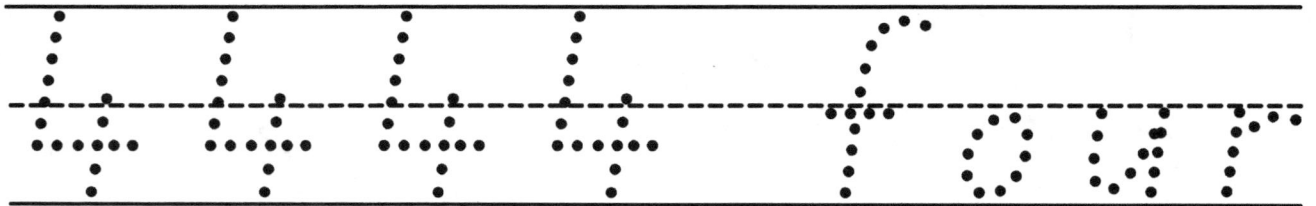

**4**

four

4 4 4 4

4 4 4 4 four

COLOR FOUR HEARTS:

CIRCLE THE FOURS:

| | | |
|---|---|---|
| 1 | 2 | 3 |
| 4 | 5 | 4 |
| 3 | 1 | 2 |
| 4 | 3 | 5 |
| 2 | 1 | 4 |

# Number Hunt

**Find and color number 4**

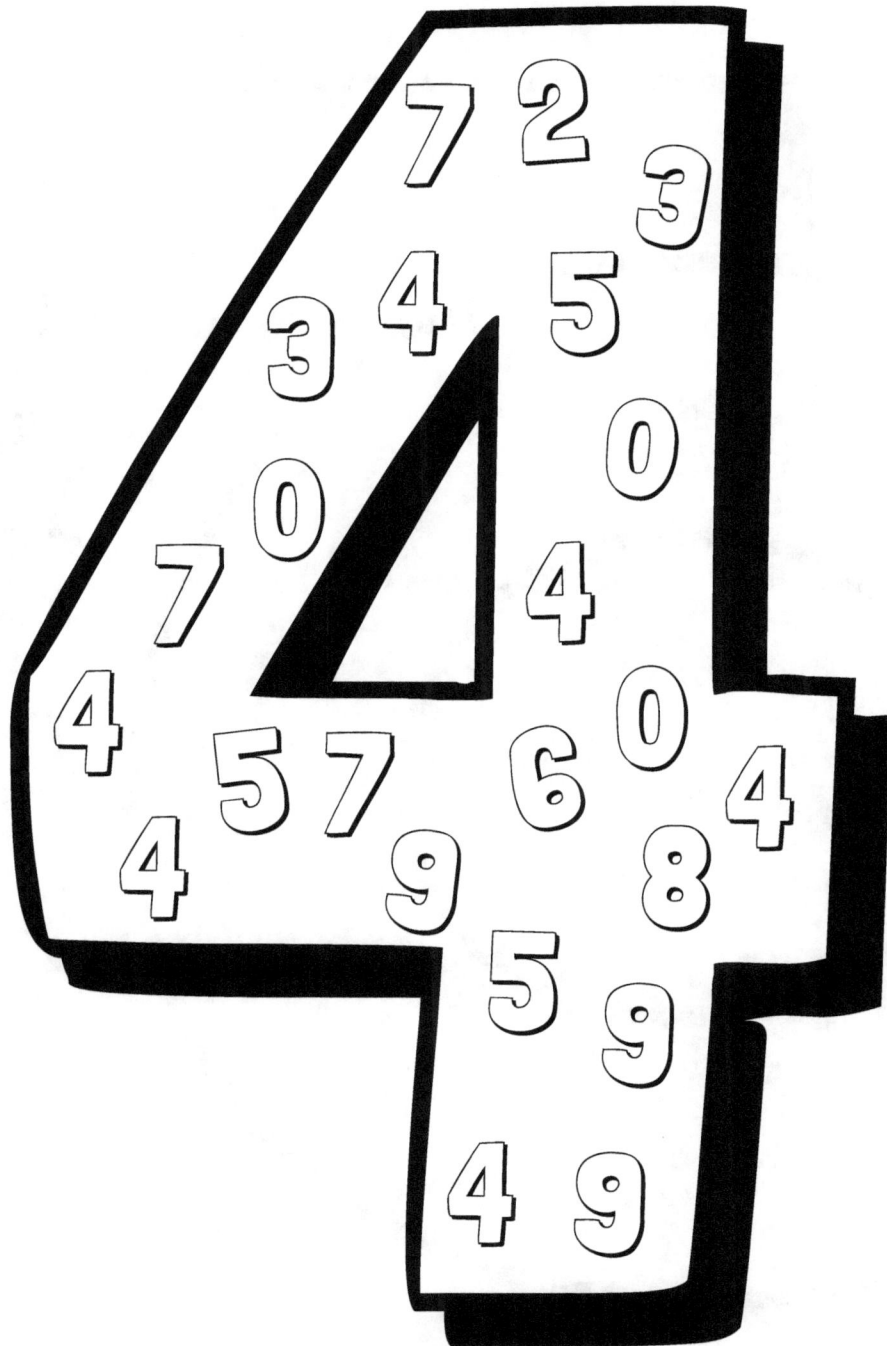

# Coloring Numbers

# Writing Numbers

## 5

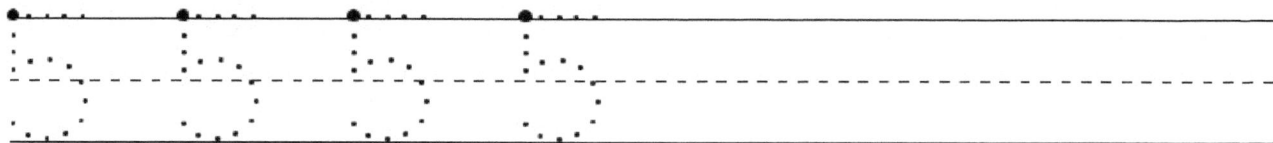

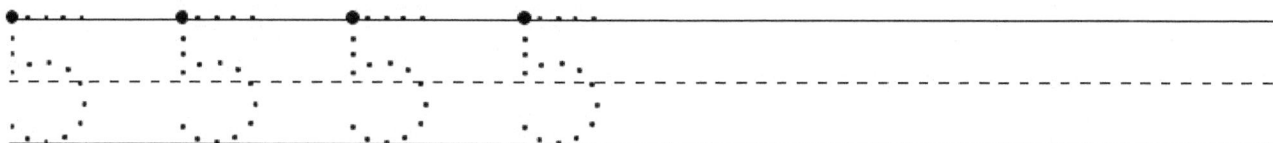

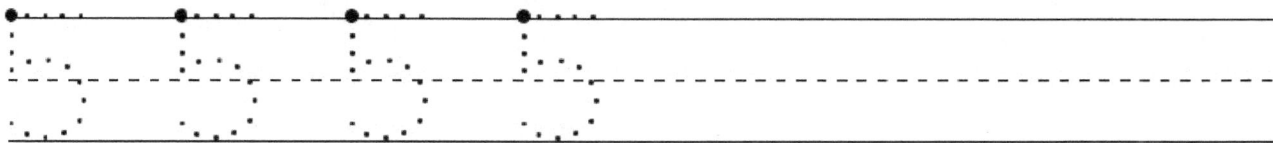

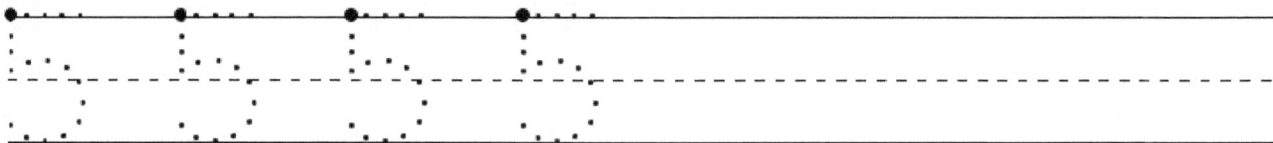

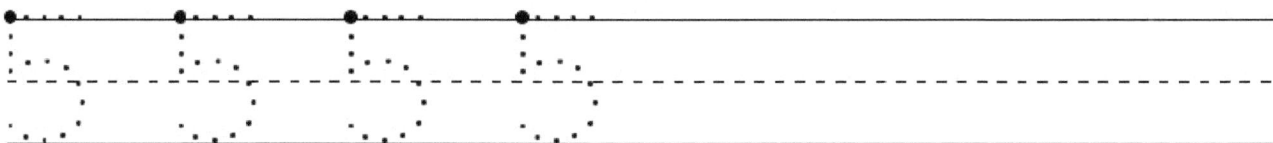

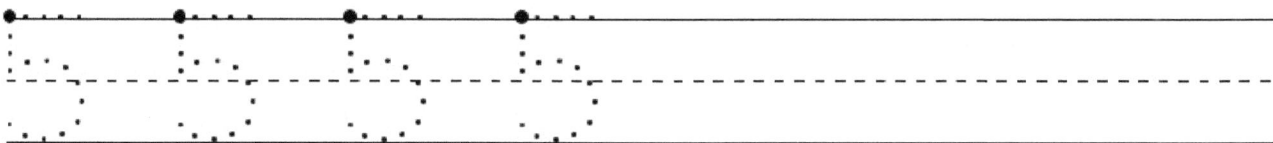

# Writing Number Words

# five

five five five

five five five

five five five

five five five

five five five

five five five

# Writing Numbers

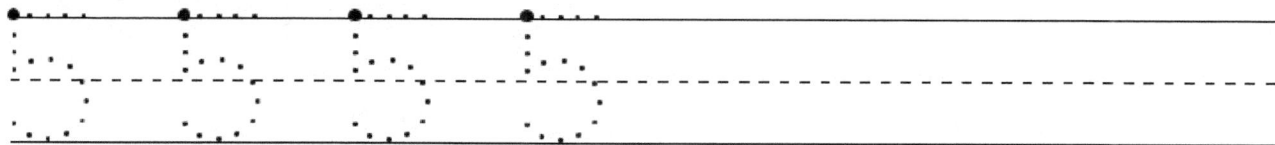

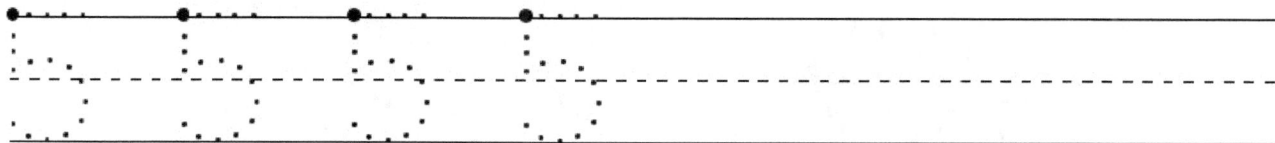

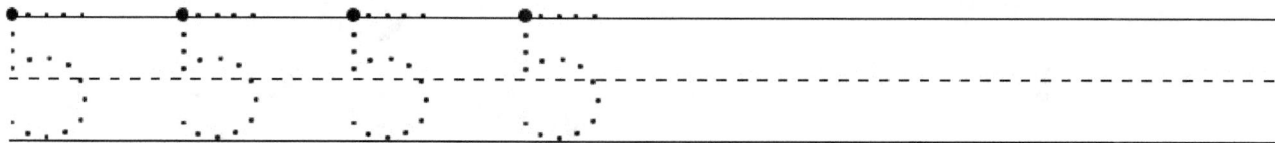

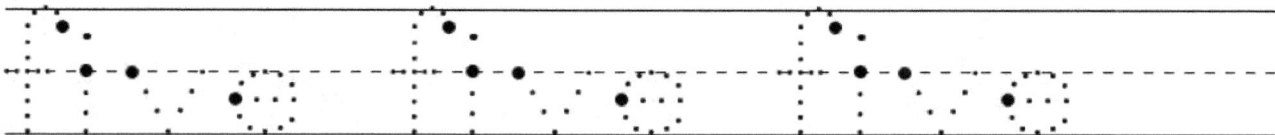

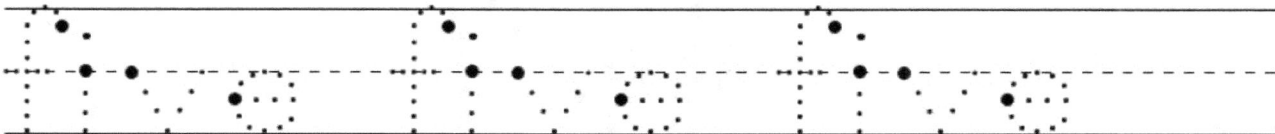

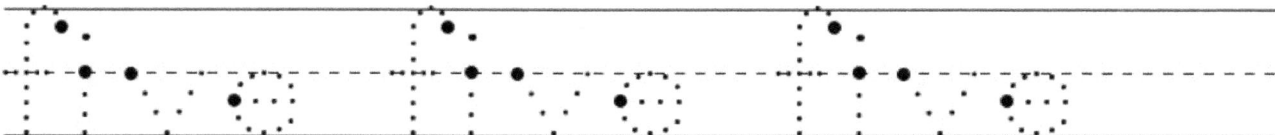

5 5 5 5

5 5 5 5

5 5 5 5

five  five  five

five  five  five

five  five  five

Coloring Objects

five

# DIRECTIONS: TRACE THE WORDS AND NUMBERS BELOW.

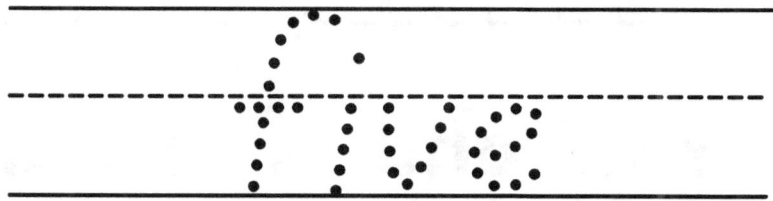

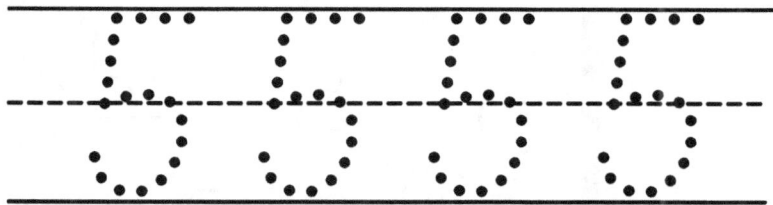

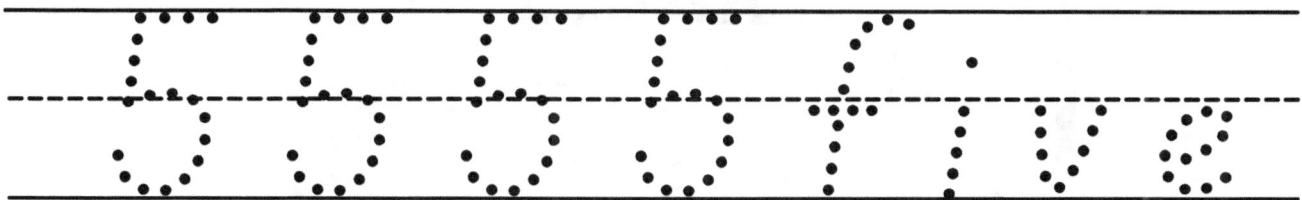

**5**

five

5 5 5 5

5 5 5 5 five

| COLOR FIVE CIRCLES | CIRCLE THE FIVES |
|---|---|
| ○ ○ ○<br>○ ○ ○<br>○ ○ ○ | 5 2 3<br>1 5 4<br>3 5 2<br>4 3 5<br>2 5 4 |

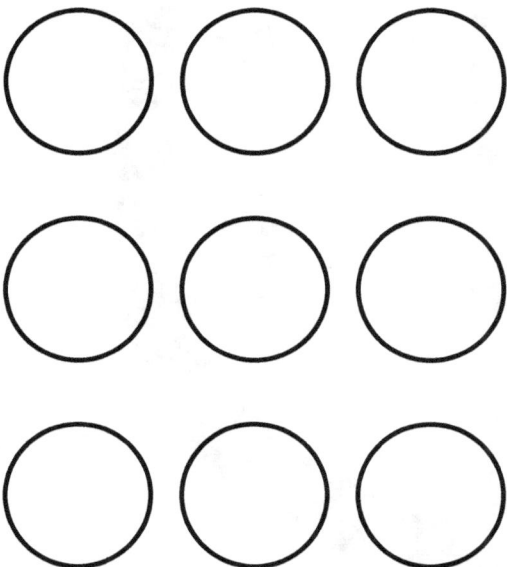

# Number Hunt

## Find and color number 5

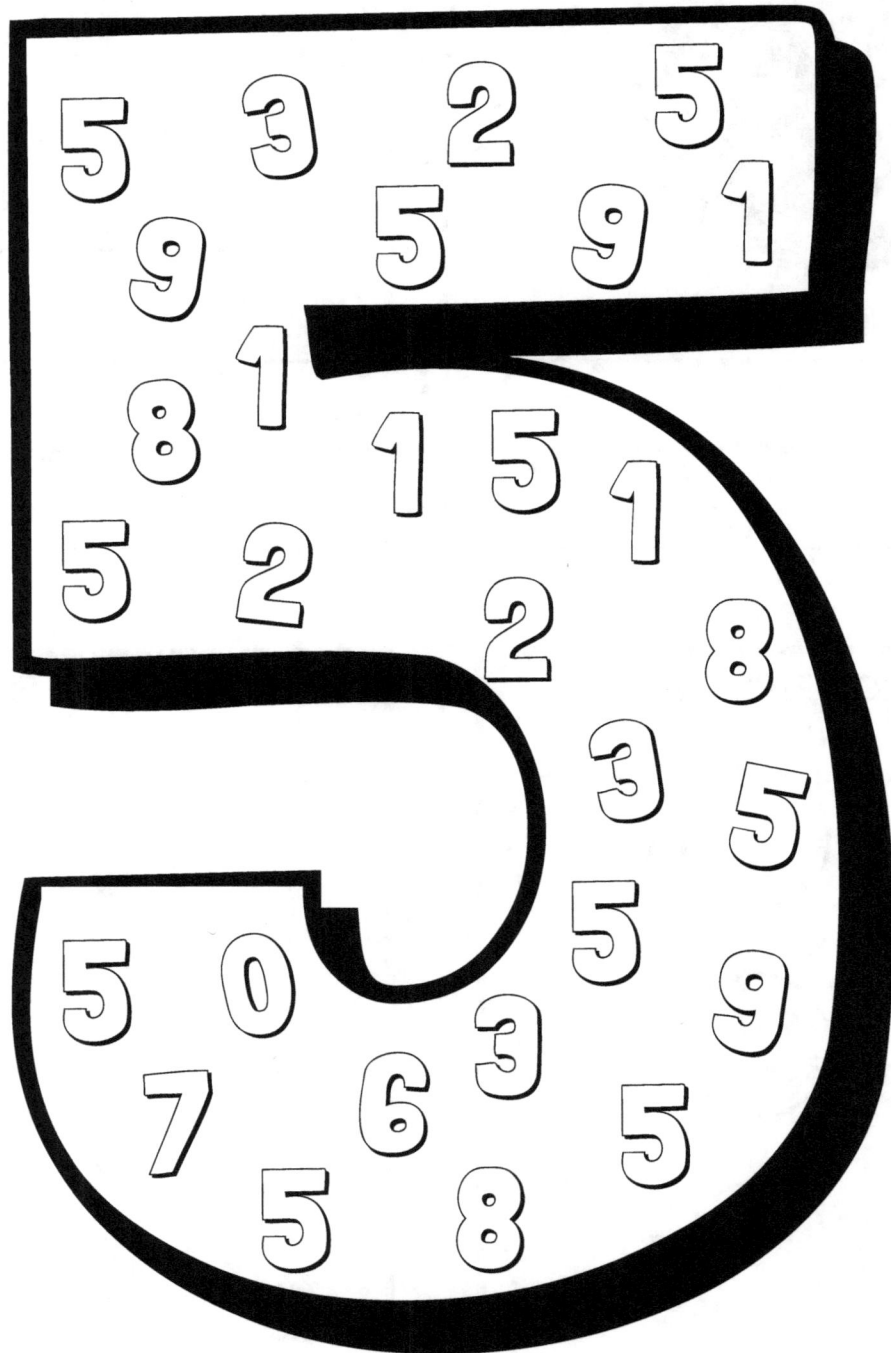

# TRACE THE NUMBERS

| | |
|---|---|
| 1 |  |
| 2 |  |
| 3 |  |
| 4 |  |
| 5 | 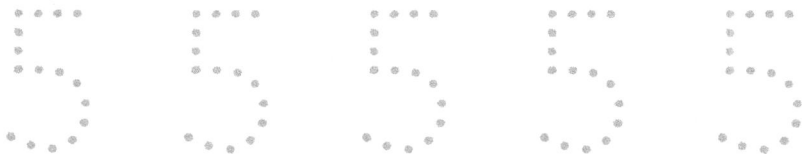 |

# Bella's Word Search

Circle the words you find from the word list below. Every word is used only one time and some of the letters are used more than one time.

```
t  r  u  o  f  e
h  u  u  x  n  v
r  e  i  i  e  i
e  s  n  n  b  f
e  e  o  t  w  o
s  e  v  e  n  z
```

# Coloring Numbers

6

# Writing Numbers 6

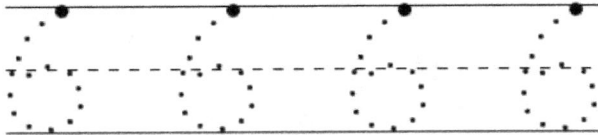

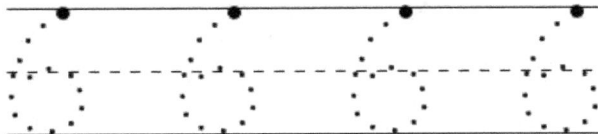

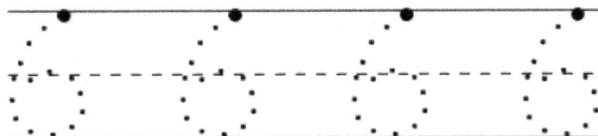

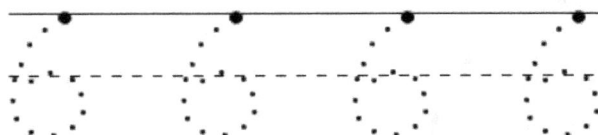

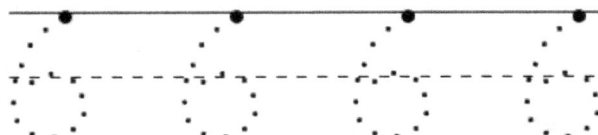

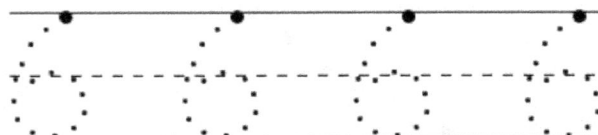

# Writing Number Words

## six

six six six

six six six

six six six

six six six

six six six

six six six

six six six

# Writing Numbers

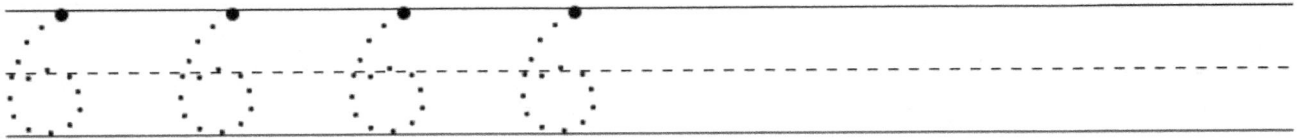

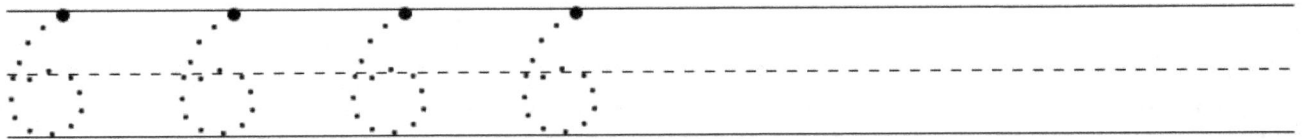

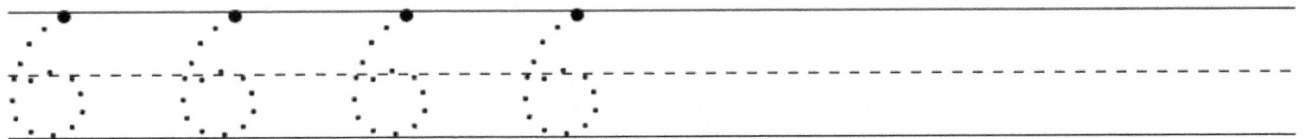

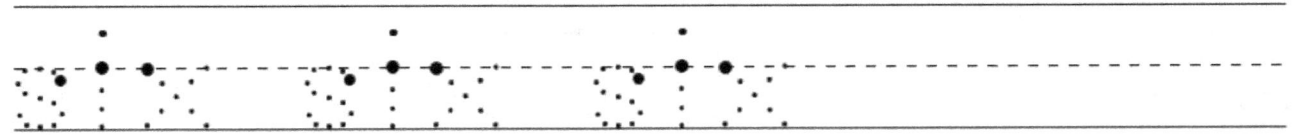

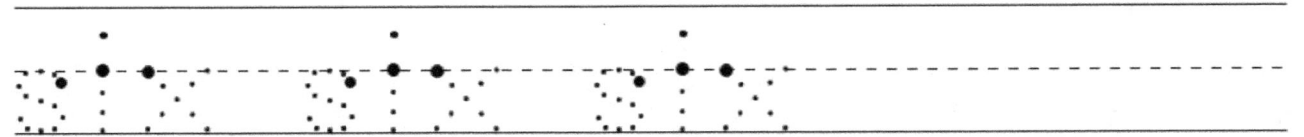

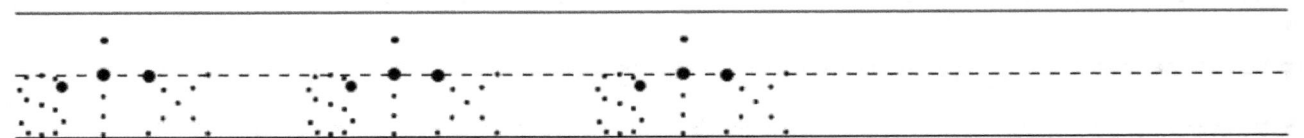

6 6 6 6

6 6 6 6

6 6 6 6

six six six

six six six

six six six

# Coloring Objects

# six

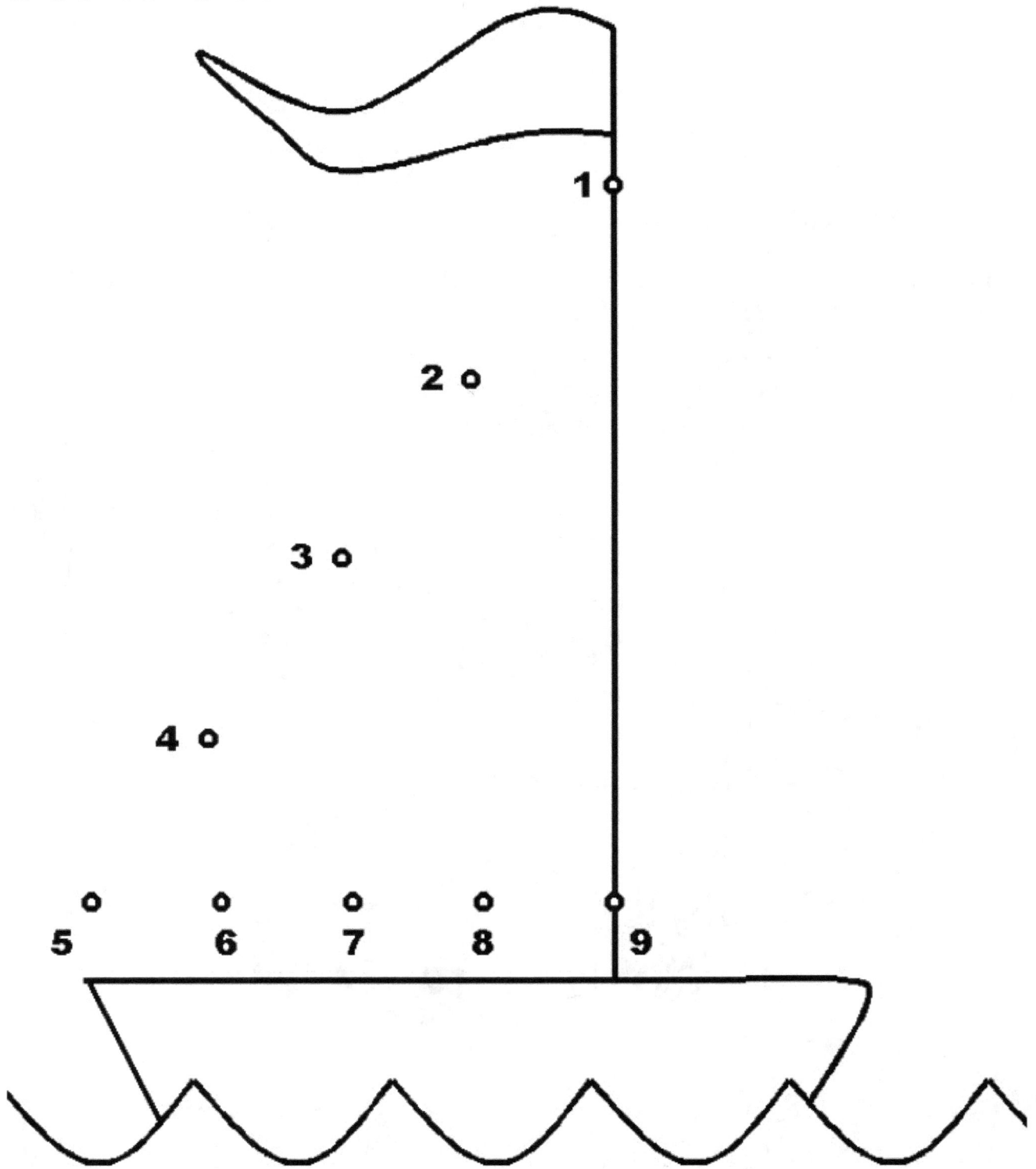

# Dot-to-Dot

**1** o

**2** o

**3** o

**4** o

o          o          o          o          o
**5**      **6**      **7**      **8**      **9**

DIRECTIONS: TRACE THE WORDS AND NUMBERS BELOW.

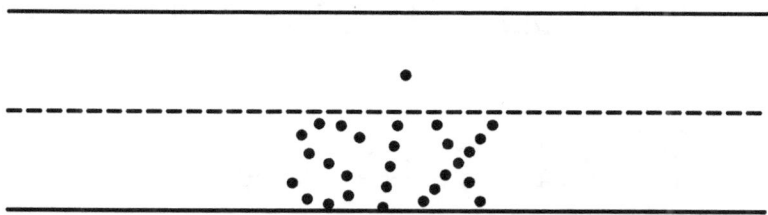

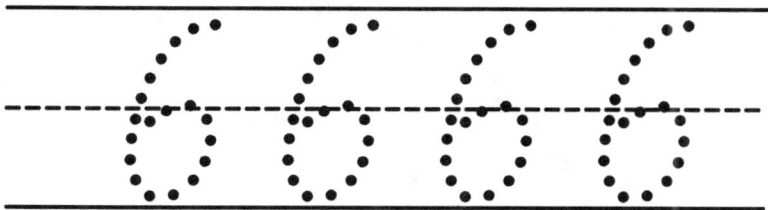

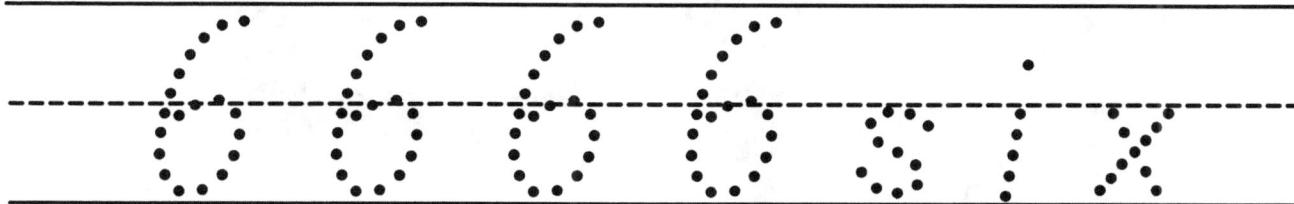

6

six

6 6 6 6

6 6 6 6 six

COLOR SIX TRIANGLES:

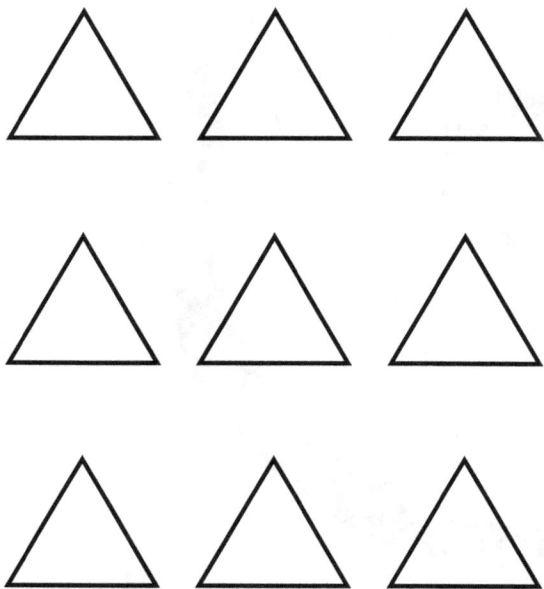

CIRCLE THE SIXES

| 5 | 6 | 3 |
|---|---|---|
| 1 | 2 | 6 |
| 6 | 5 | 4 |
| 4 | 3 | 6 |
| 2 | 6 | 1 |

# Number Hunt

## Find and color number 6

# Coloring Numbers

7

# Writing Numbers 7

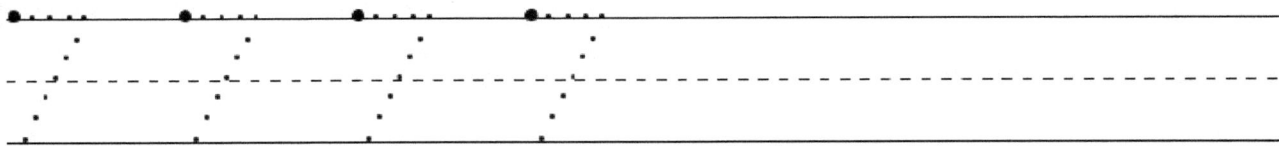

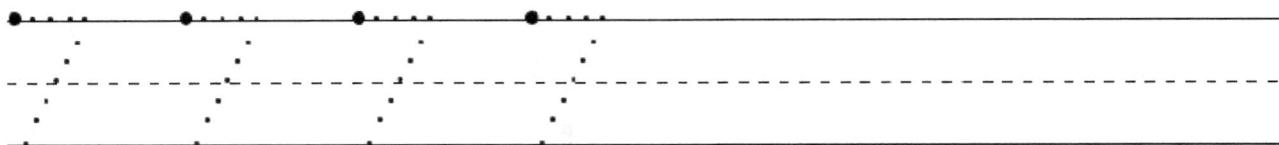

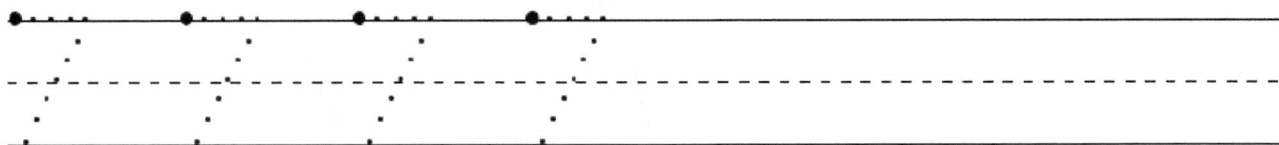

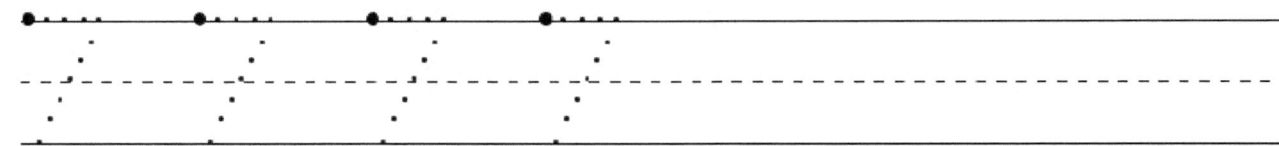

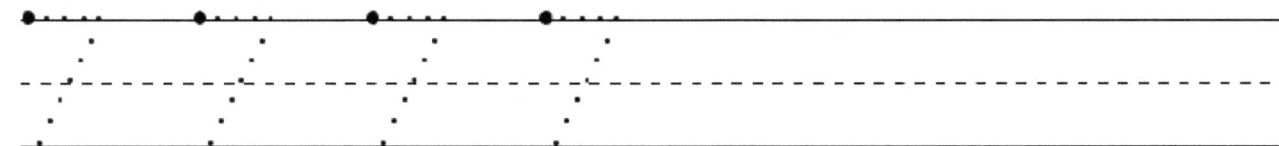

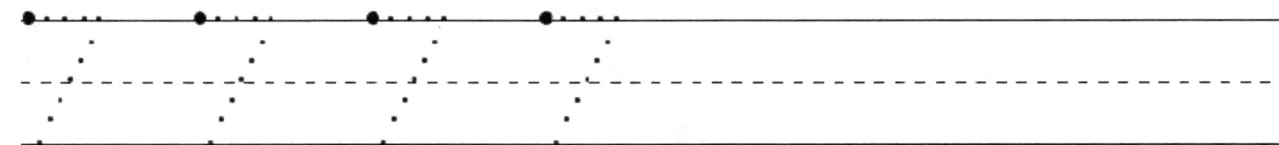

# Writing Number Words

seven

seven seven

seven seven

seven seven

seven seven

seven seven

seven seven

seven seven

# Writing Numbers

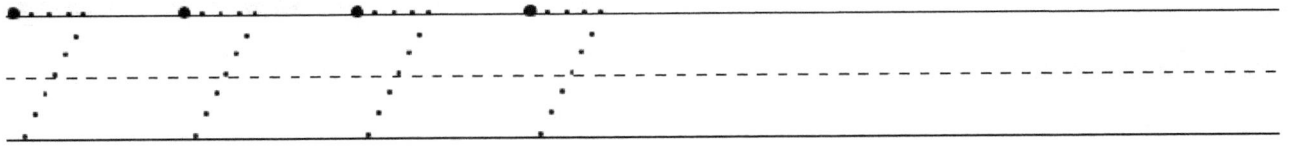

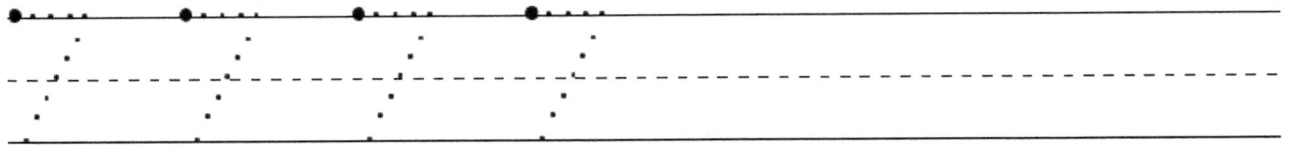

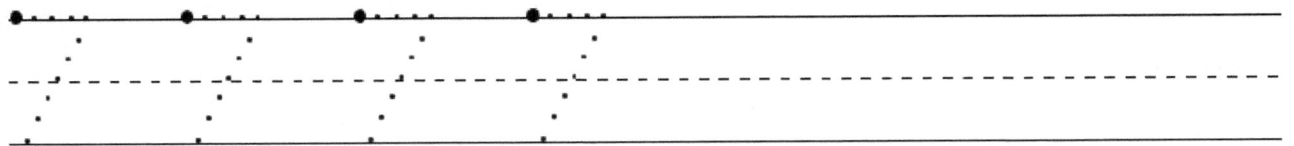

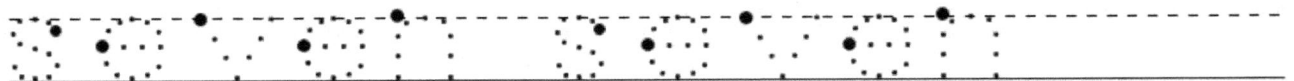

7 7 7 7

7 7 7 7

7 7 7 7

seven seven

seven seven

seven seven

# Coloring Objects

seven

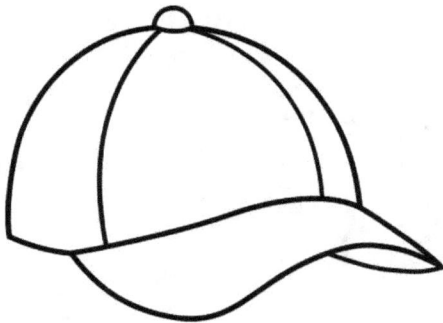

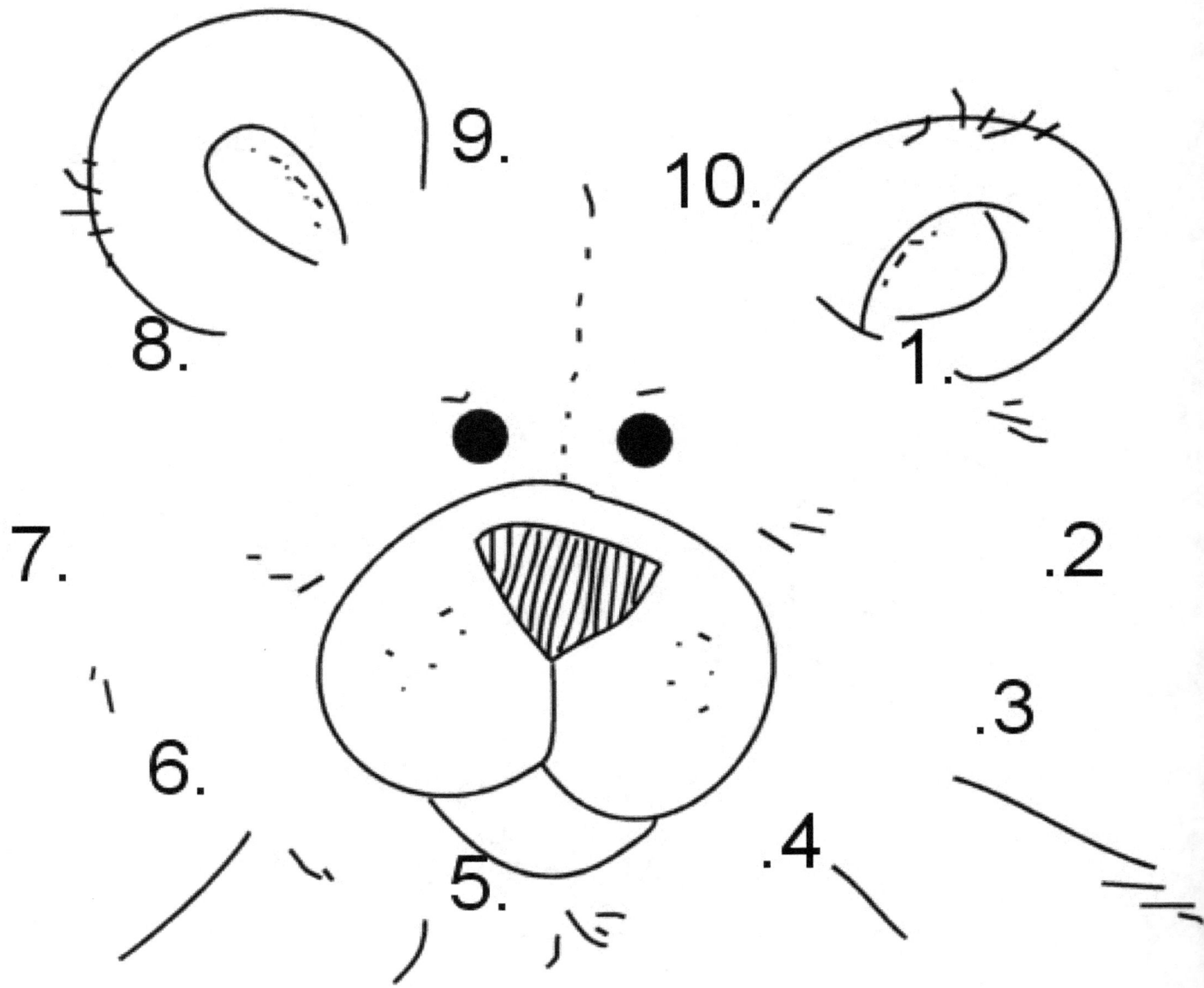

# Dot-to-Dot

9.

10.

8.

1.

7.

.2

6.

.3

.4

5.

# DIRECTIONS: TRACE THE WORDS AND NUMBERS BELOW.

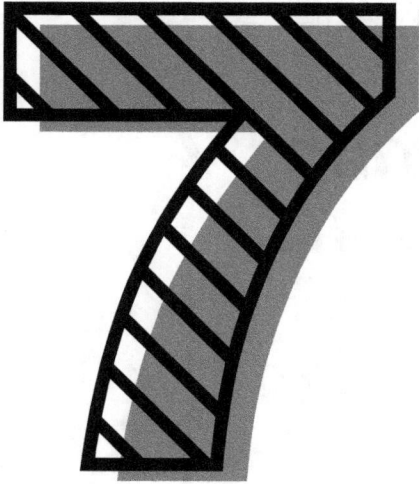

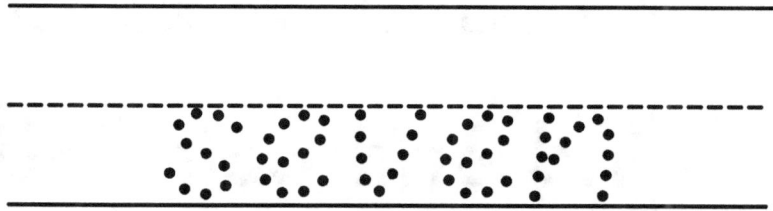

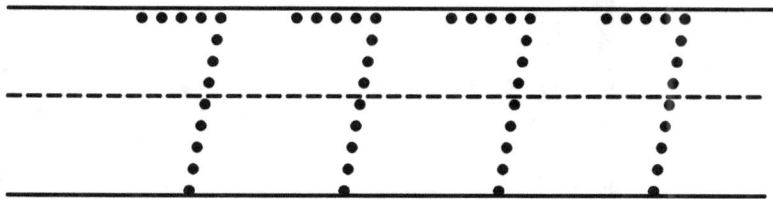

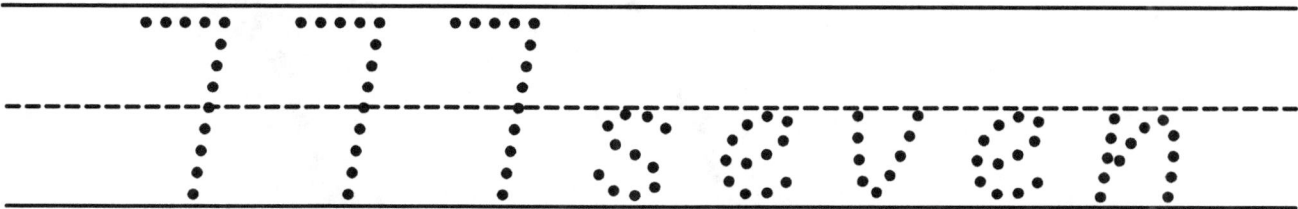

**7**

seven

7777

777 seven

---

**COLOR SEVEN HEXAGONS**

**CIRCLE THE SEVENS**

| 5 | 7 | 3 |
| 1 | 7 | 4 |
| 7 | 3 | 2 |
| 4 | 2 | 7 |
| 7 | 5 | 4 |

# Number Hunt

## Find and color number 7

7 1 4 0
2 3 2 7
2 0
7
1 5
4
5
2
7 1
6 8

# Coloring Numbers

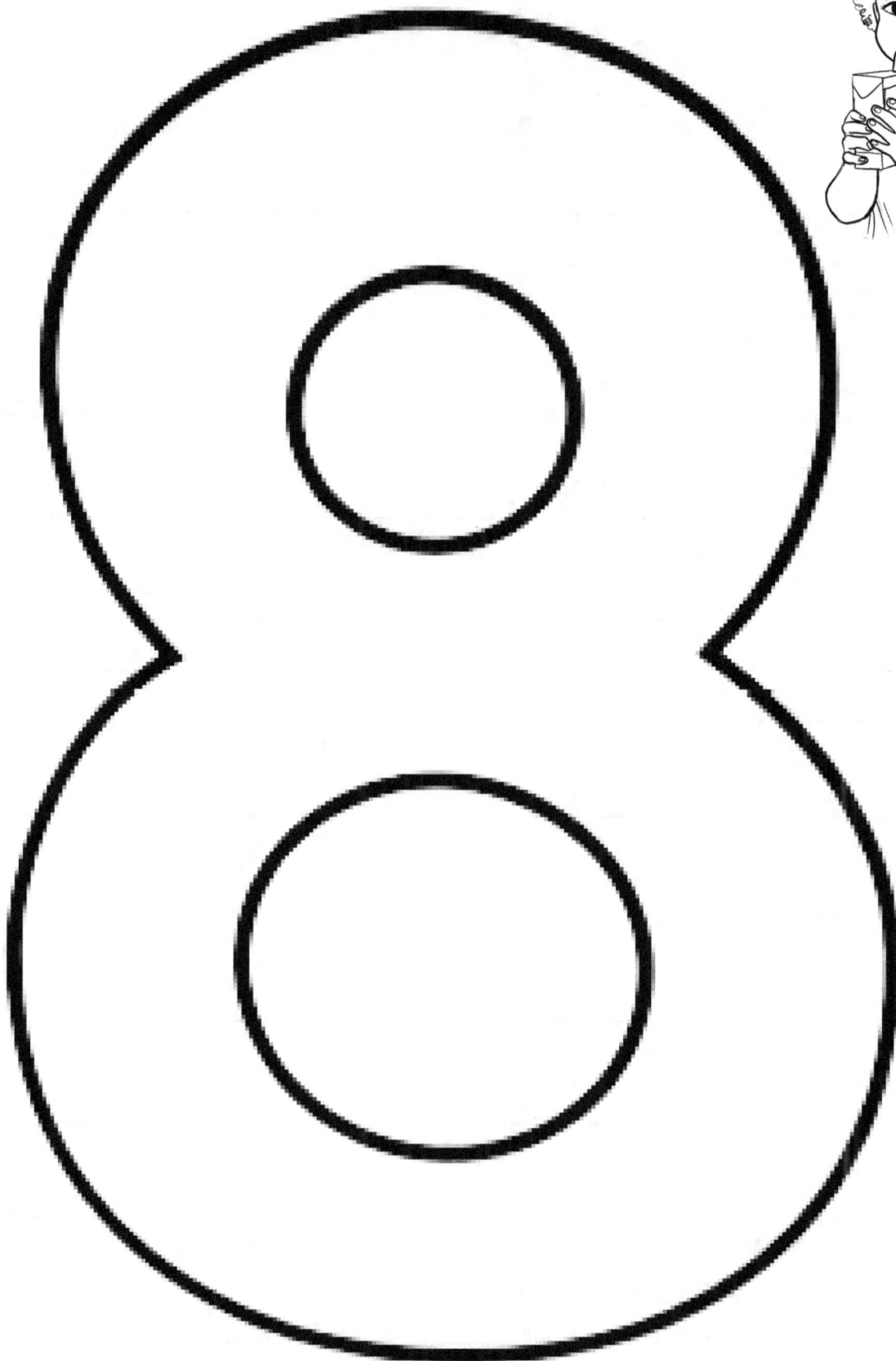

8

# Writing Numbers 8

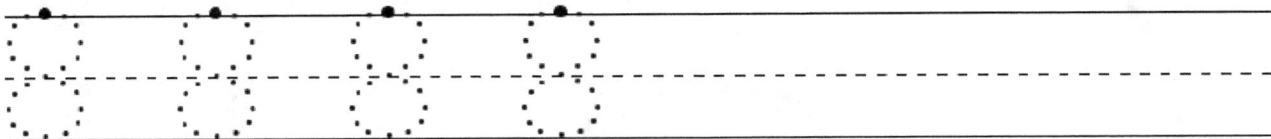

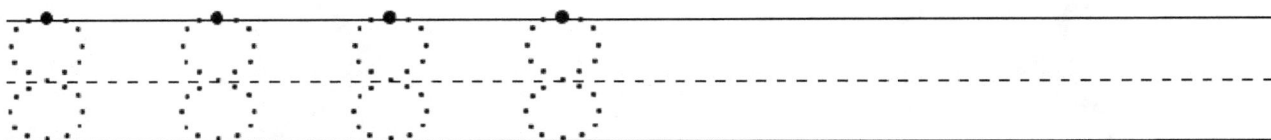

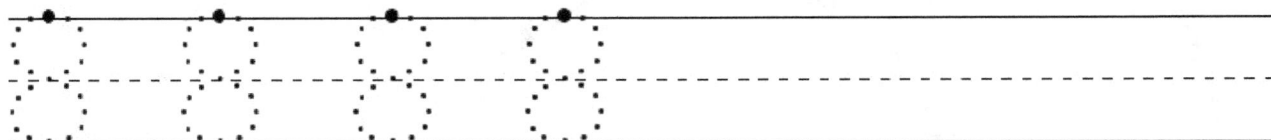

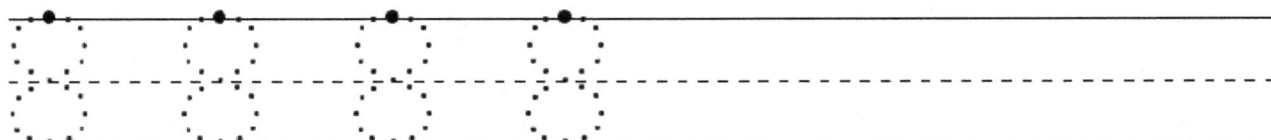

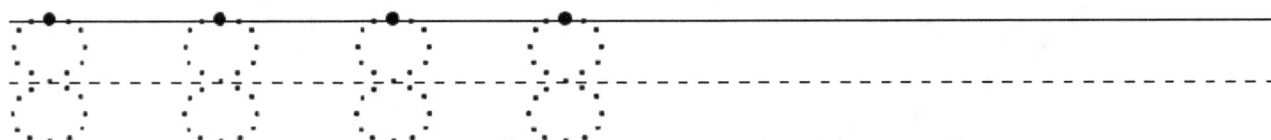

# Writing Number Words

## eight

eight eight

eight eight

eight eight

eight eight

eight eight

eight eight

# Writing Numbers

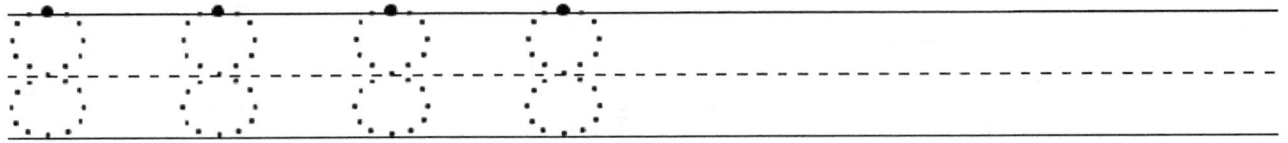

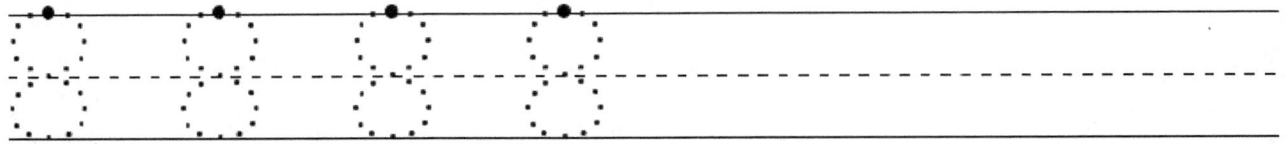

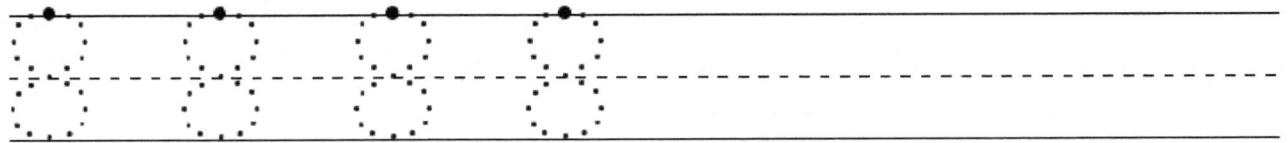

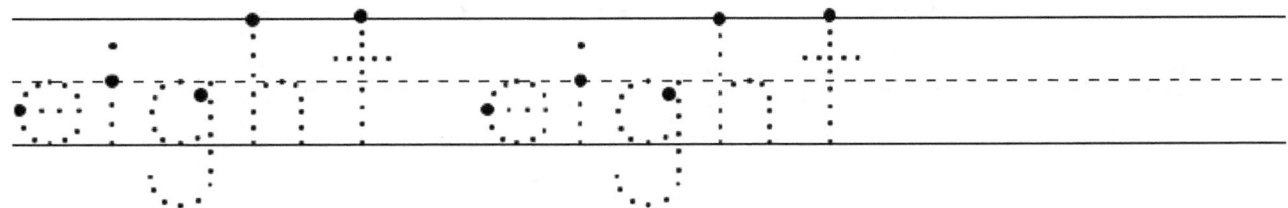

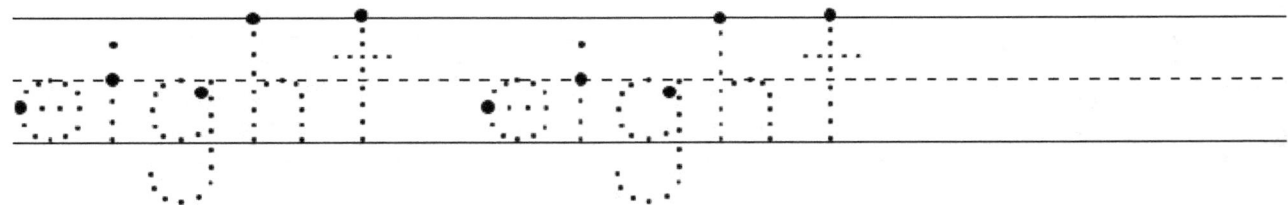

8  8  8  8

8  8  8  8

8  8  8  8

eight eight

eight eight

eight eight

# Coloring Objects

# eight

# Dot-to-Dot

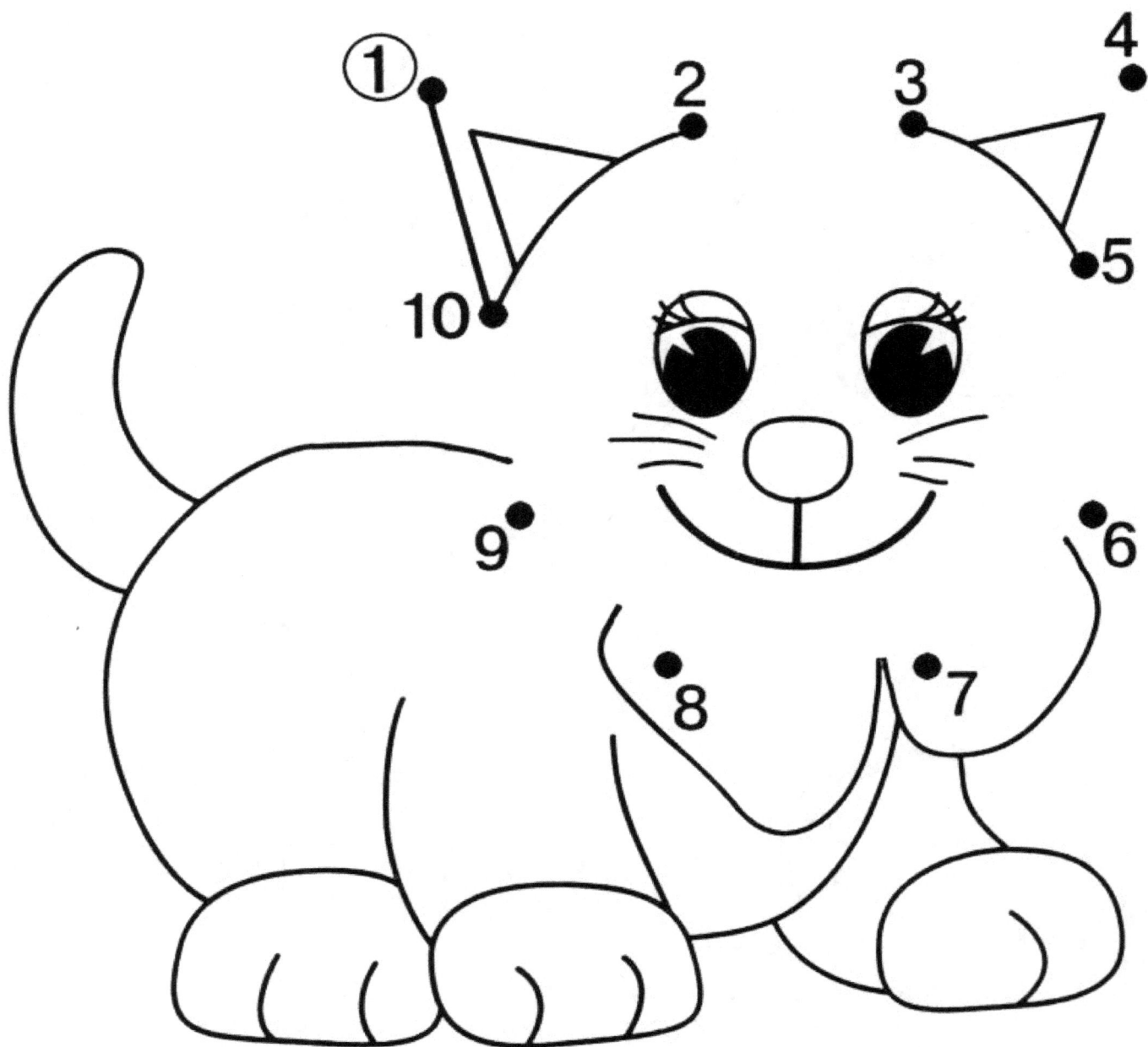

DIRECTIONS:  TRACE THE WORDS AND NUMBERS BELOW.

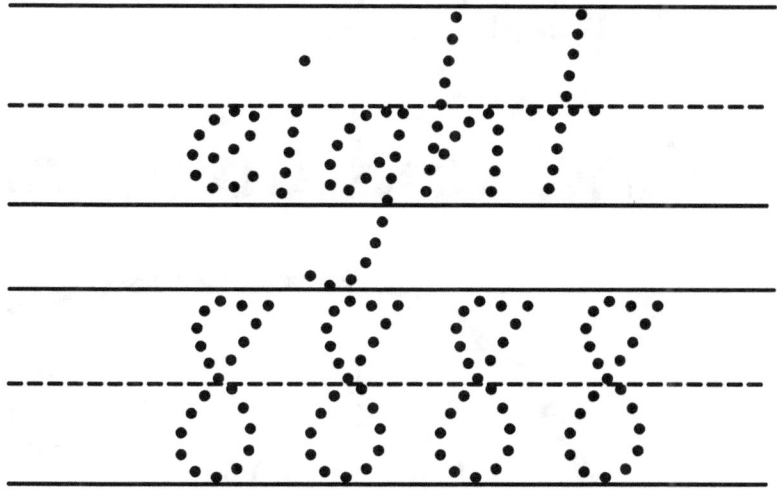

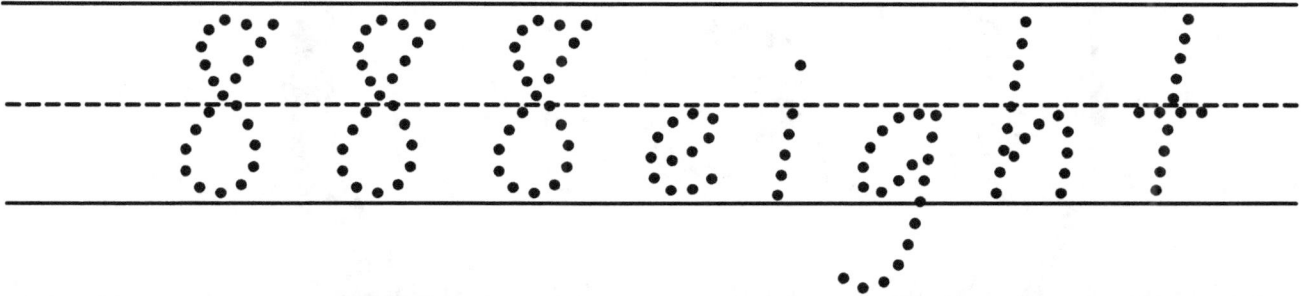

**8**

eight

8 8 8
8 8 8

8 8 8 eight

COLOR EIGHT DIAMONDS:

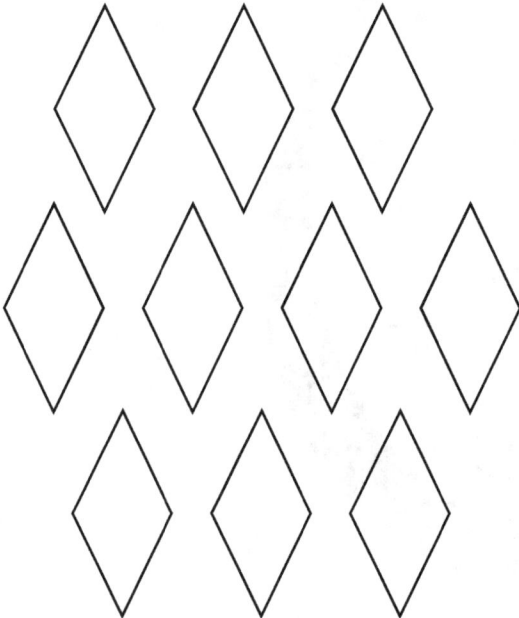

CIRCLE THE EIGHTS:

| | | |
|---|---|---|
| 1 | 8 | 3 |
| 4 | 5 | 8 |
| 8 | 6 | 2 |
| 4 | 3 | 8 |
| 2 | 5 | 1 |

# Number Hunt

## Find and color number 8

# Coloring Numbers

9

# Writing Numbers 9

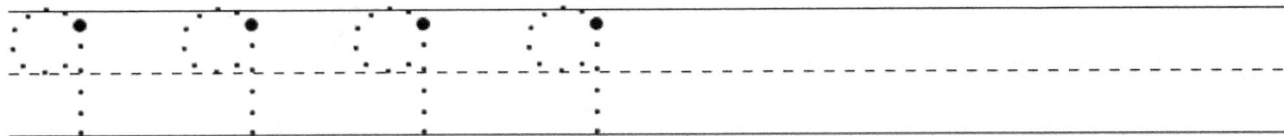

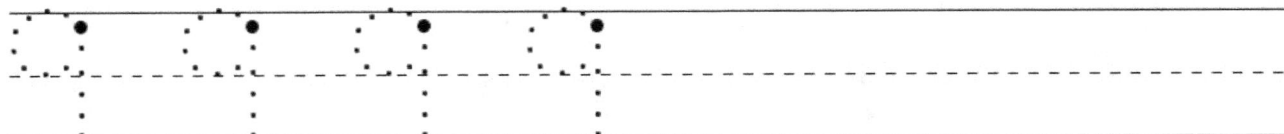

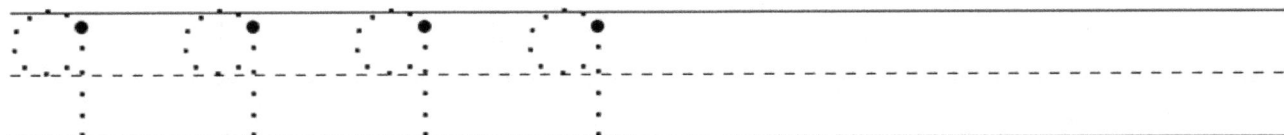

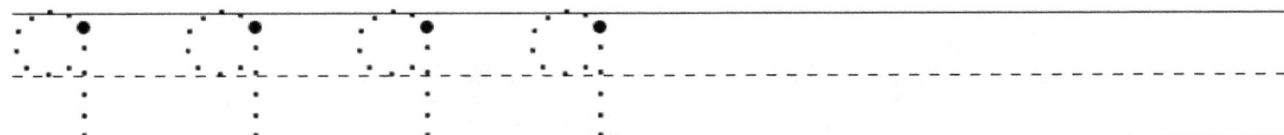

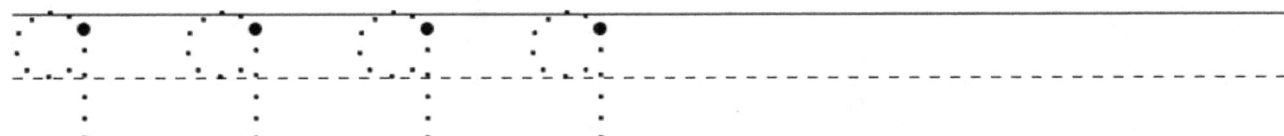

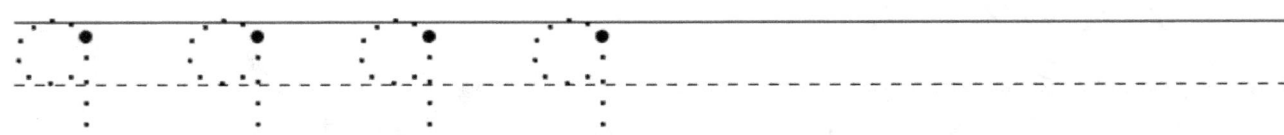

# Writing Number Words

## nine

nine nine nine nine

nine nine nine

nine nine nine

nine nine nine

nine nine nine

nine nine nine

# Writing Numbers

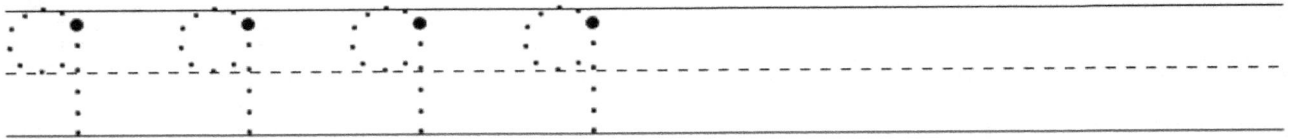

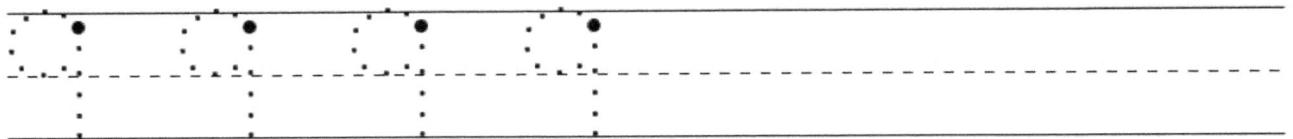

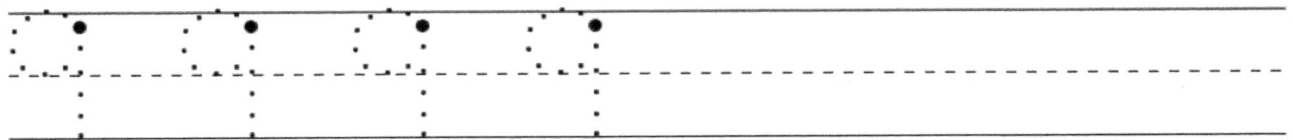

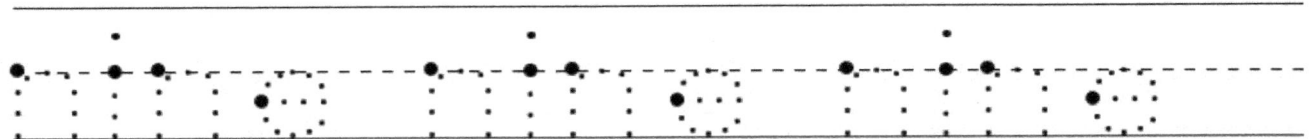

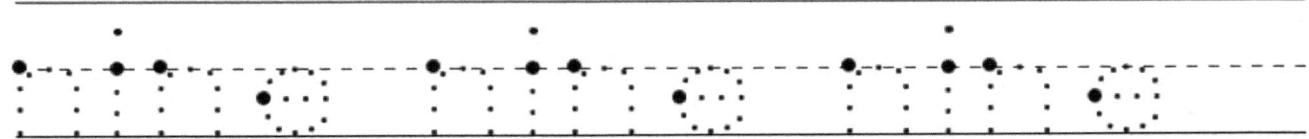

9 9 9 9

9 9 9 9

9 9 9 9

nine nine nine

nine nine nine

nine nine nine

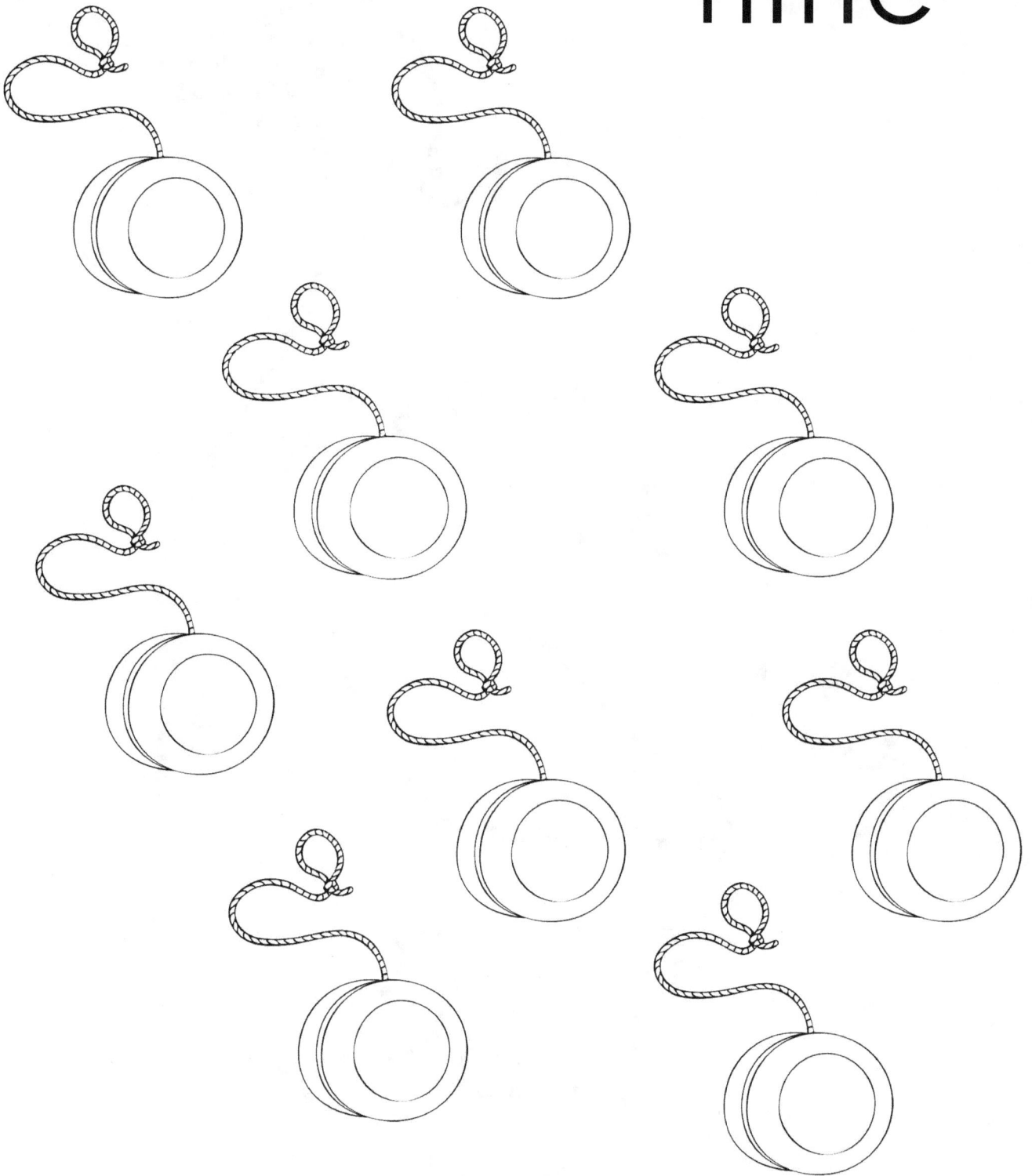

# Coloring Objects

nine

# Dot-to-Dot

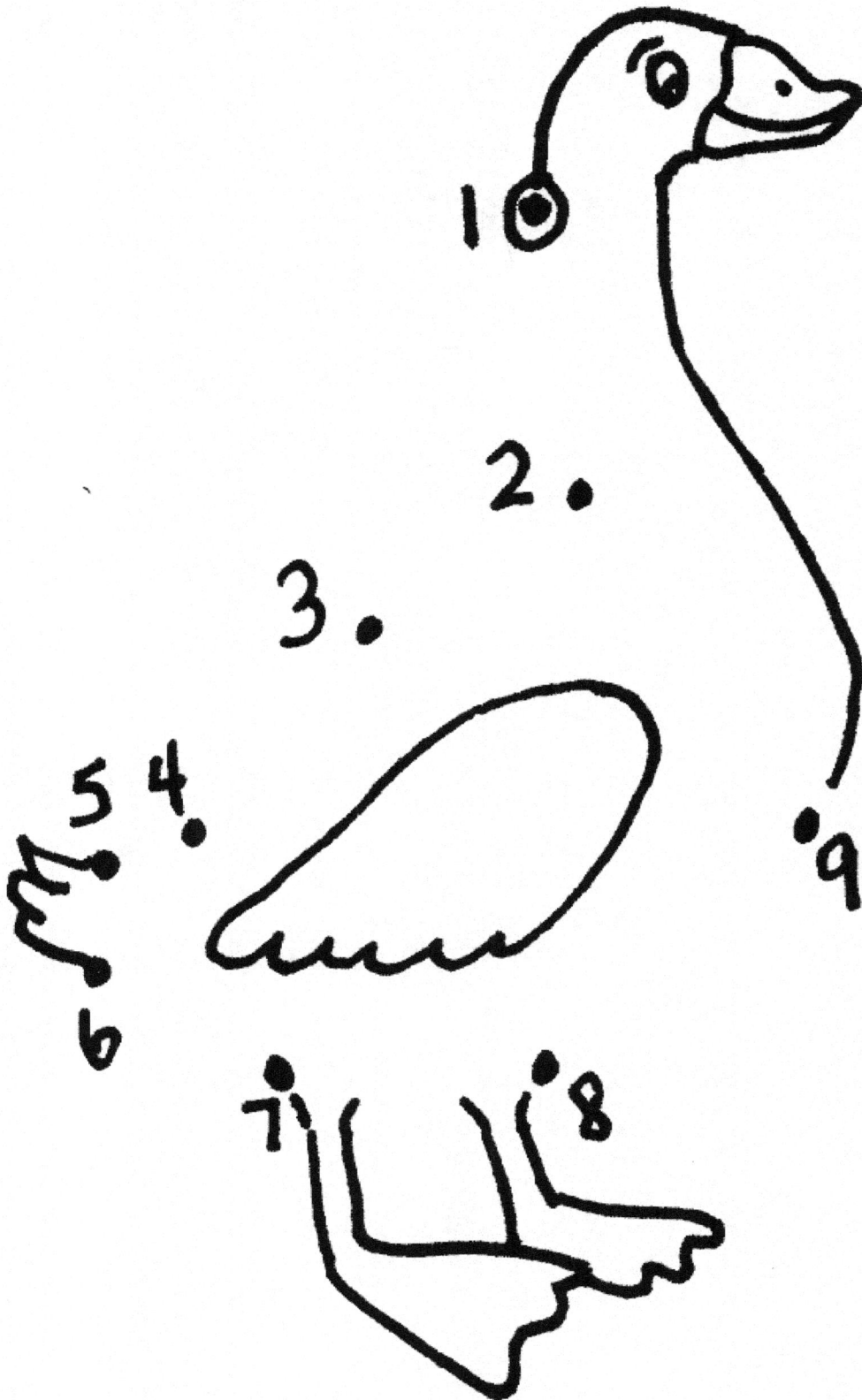

DIRECTIONS: TRACE THE WORDS AND NUMBERS BELOW.

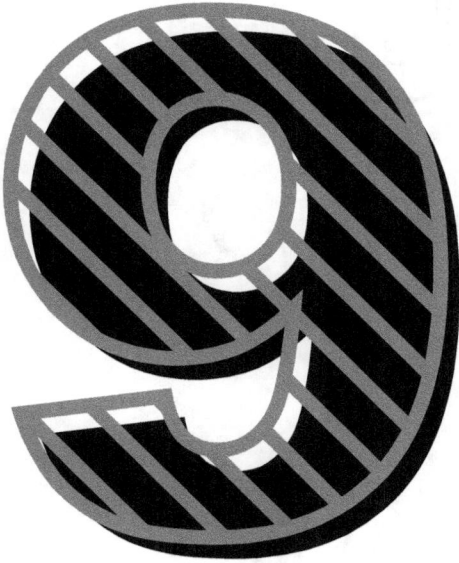

9

nine

9 9 9 9

9 9 9 9 nine

COLOR NINE HATS:

CIRCLE THE NINES:

| 9 | 8 | 6 |
|---|---|---|
| 4 | 7 | 9 |
| 8 | 6 | 9 |
| 4 | 9 | 8 |
| 9 | 5 | 1 |

# Number Hunt

## Find and color number 9

9

0 1 8
0 5 9 2
2 4 9
5 2 8
7 9 5 4
8 4 9 8 9
9
8 9
8 7 6
6 7 0 8
1 9 9 7 8

# Coloring Numbers

10

# Writing Numbers 10

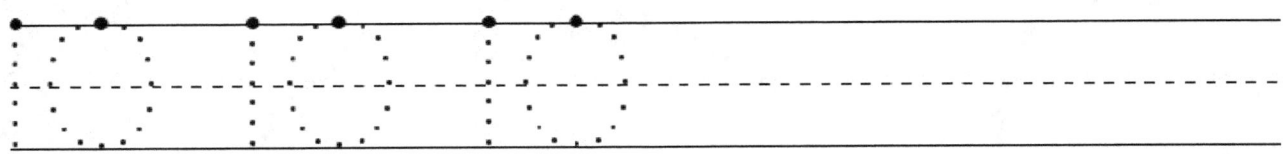

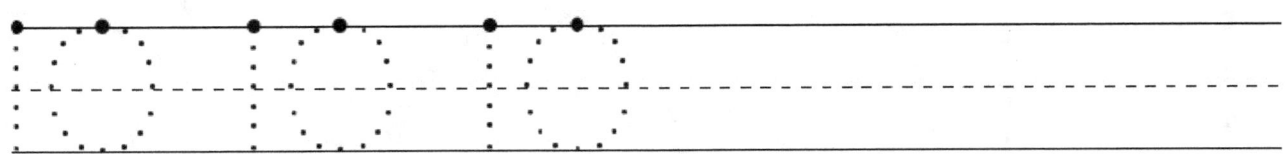

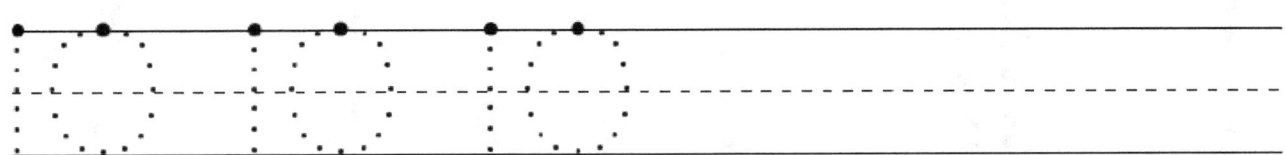

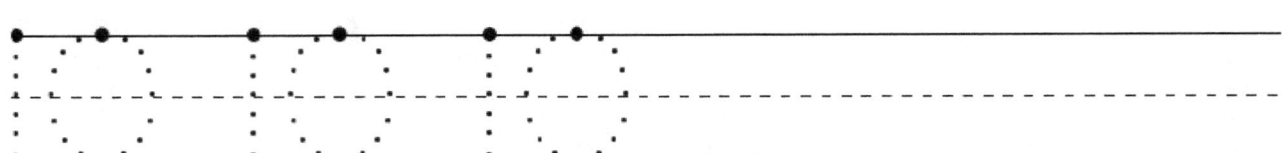

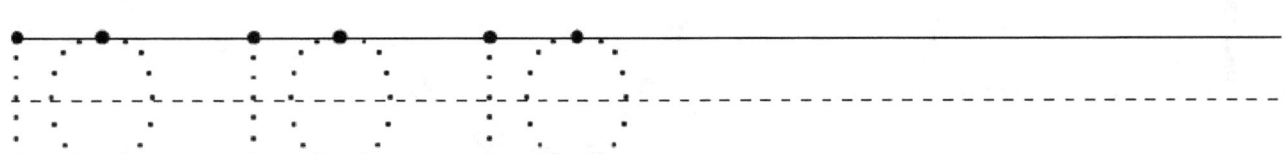

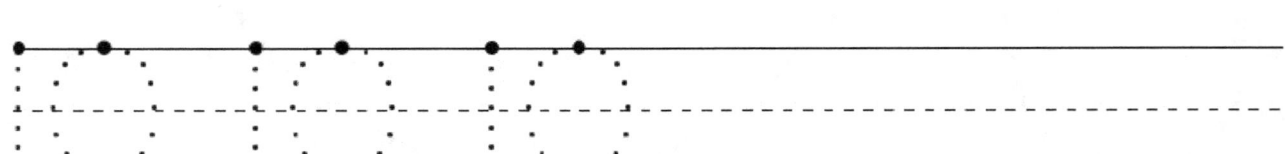

# Writing Number Words

## ten

ten ten ten

ten ten ten

ten ten ten

ten ten ten

ten ten ten

ten ten ten

# Writing Numbers

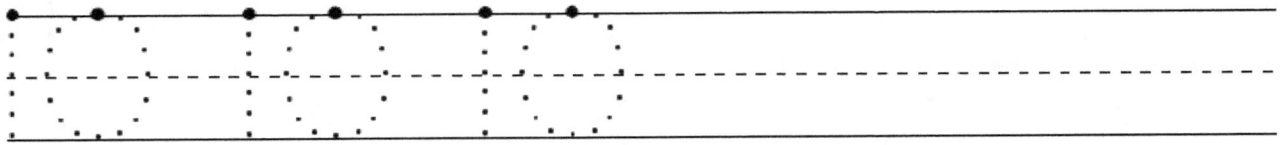

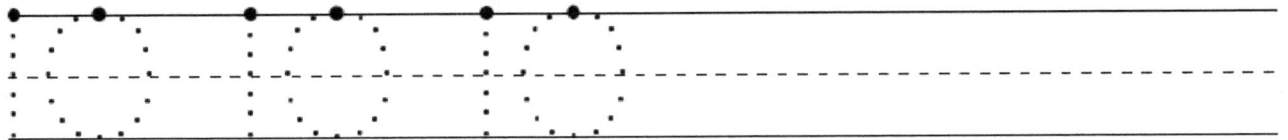

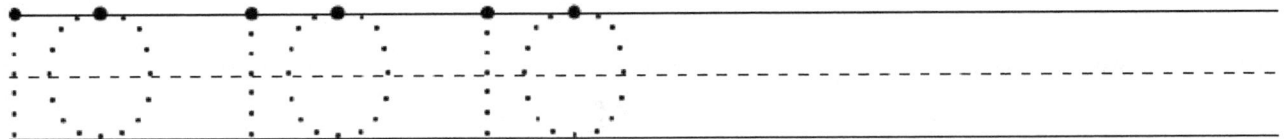

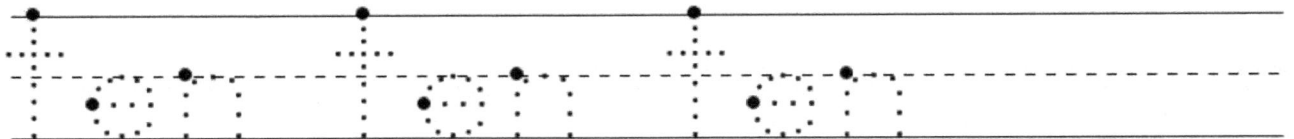

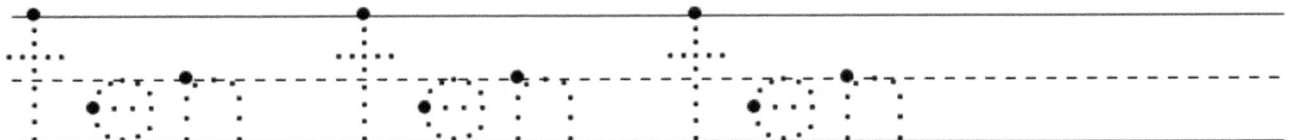

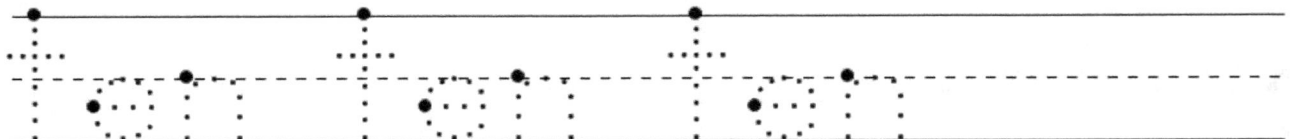

10 10 10

10 10 10

10 10 10

ten ten ten

ten ten ten

ten ten ten

# Coloring Objects

# ten

# Coloring Numbers 1-3

# Coloring Numbers 4-6

# Coloring Numbers 7-10

# Coloring Numbers 1-5

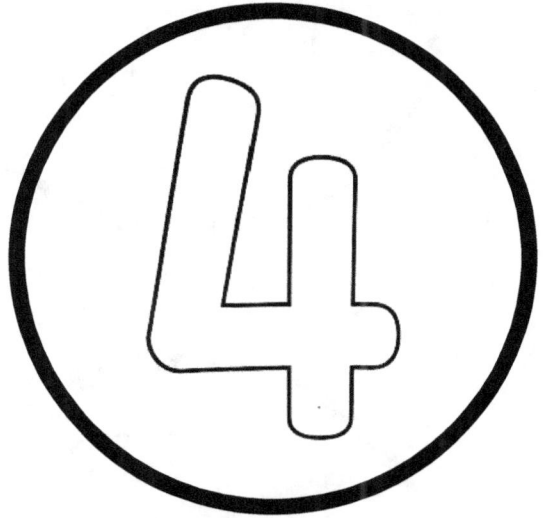

1

2

3

4

5

# Coloring Numbers 6-10

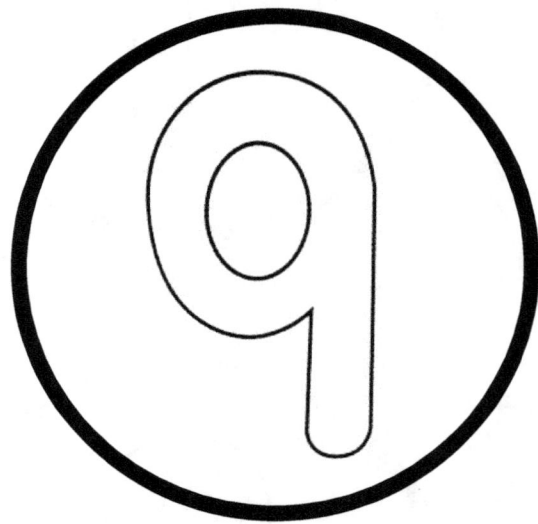

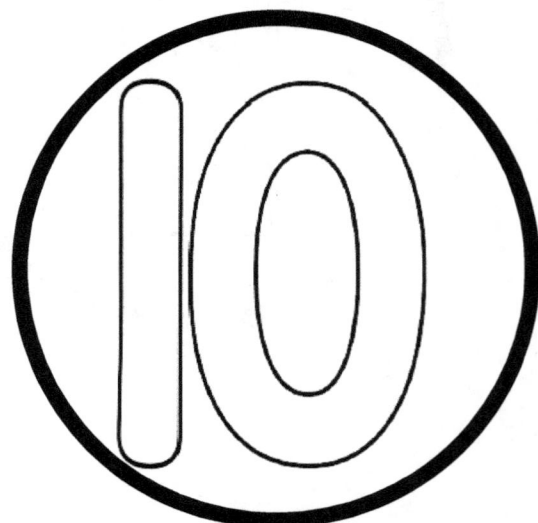

6

7

8

9

10

# How Many?

 ☐  ☐  ☐

# How Many?

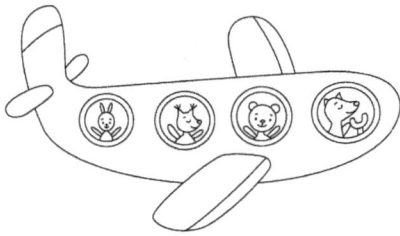

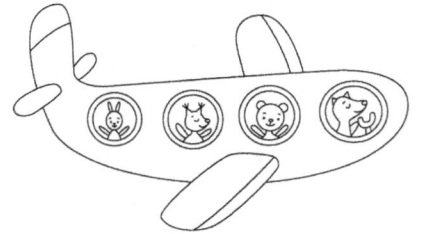

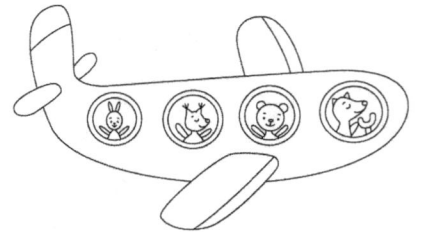

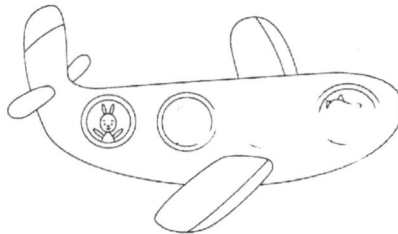

# How Many?